Me and the Ugly C

D1382652

By

Becky Dennington

LAZY DAY
PUBLISHING

www.lazydaypub.com

Me and the Ugly C

Digital ISBN- 9781612580401
Print ISBN- 1-61258-040-8

ALL RIGHTS RESERVED
Copyright © 2011 Becky Dennington
Cover art by Bret Poinier
Cover Photo by Julie Dodd

No part of this book may be used or reproduced in any manner whatsoever without the express written permission from the publisher LazyDay, with the exception of quotes used in reviews and critical articles.

Dedication

For Kelley – my knight in shining armor, my hero, and my best friend
For Ryan and Mallory – the loves of my life and the very reasons I breathe

INTRODUCTION

I always said I was going to be a writer someday. Have my picture on the back of a book and my name on the front. Maybe I'd use one of those fake author names. A super fun one like Penelope Huffnagle or Lily Arugula.

But what would I write about? A love story? An exciting adventure book geared toward kids? A thriller with a murderous plot? The problem is, well, I'm just really not that cool. I'm terrible at witty retorts and although I find myself hilarious, most of the time I stand alone. So how can I create characters that say cool things or sparkle in the sunlight and make all the girls swoon or go to wizard school and say cool spells that turn on the lights or lift things into the air? Lumos! Leviosa!

I could go on and on but what I'm getting at is that I'm 36 now. I'm not famous like I totally thought I was going to be. I really expected for Oprah to have called by now and the movies made from the series of books I had written about some magical universe where humans have wings or where two star-crossed lovers chase each other through time and space as they battle good and evil while healing the sick and feeding the hungry should surely be taking the box-office by storm.

So, ok, fiction isn't my bag. How about real life? I could write about something that really happened. It's like cheating a little though. How creative is that to write about what happened to me today? I mean, who is going to want to read that? Or BUY it for that matter? That's too much pressure. And frankly, truth be told, I'm so scattered I can't focus on any one thing for too long. I had self-diagnosed myself with ADD but a friend pointed out to me that what I actually have is ADOS -- Attention Deficit Oooooohh Shiny!!!

But I DO have a story to tell, and I thought writing my story would have a lot of therapeutic value in it for me. So my solution -- a blog.

A long time ago, *Saturday Night Live* had a little skit they did called "Deep Thoughts by Jack Handey." It was just a part in the show where words scrolled across the screen and began like pure enlightenment and ended leaving you thinking, "Huh?" Here's an example.

"If you had to list the different types of haircuts in order of how warm they kept the head, you'd probably put the flat top near the bottom. But you know, I bet it's surprisingly warm."

-- "Deep Thoughts" by Jack Handey

See what I mean? Now that's deep. Ok, it amused me then, and it amuses me now. I always thought those things were hilarious. They didn't make a lick of sense, and I loved it! So I have always had a running commentary in my head of "Deep Thoughts by Beck," random musings that most likely only I would find funny or worth a giggle. But that DID sound like a good place to start.

This brought me to the beginning of my blog....*Deep Thoughts by Beck.*

Months after logging my deep thoughts onto the screen of my computer, my friend, Cory, took it upon himself to pitch the writings in my blog to a publisher. LazyDay Publishing soon after offered me a contract, and now my lifelong dream of being an author is coming true.

This is the story of me and my breast cancer. The story of *Me and the Ugly C.*

Welcome to my journey.

Chapter 1

Here's the story...

Once upon a time, I went to the gynecologist, got a Pap smear and came home with cancer. Well, not really. There's more to it than that. I don't know how detailed my ADOS is going to let me get with this, but I'm just gonna let it flow. Ahhhhh, the freedom. Anyhoo....let's continue on.

Let's talk about a Pap smear. Really, who wants to go strip down naked and let a stranger come look and examine all your stuff? Wait, maybe I don't want everyone to answer that. But as for myself, I do NOT find this enjoyable or ego-boosting. A necessity, in all honesty, I only did to get my prescription filled for the year. So I mentally went at it every year like a raging bull. Didn't think about it until appointment day. Jumped in the car and arrived promptly at said time. They call me back, and I walk boldly into the room with a confident swagger and a smile. Show no fear. They tell me "Here's your gown. Please take everything off and the gown opens in the front. This goes across your lap. The doctor will be in in a minute." I'm nonchalant and gracious. "Ok, thanks," I say as I lay my purse down. But buddy, when that door closes, I feel like I'm on a game show. I picture a big digital clock on the wall counting down with racing seconds. Shoes come off first while I speedily remove my clothes and grab the gown. But this is not a gown. I repeat......this is NOT A GOWN! It's a large napkin with arm holes cut out. But what a relief it is to have it on. Then I grab my clothes. They must be folded! All unmentionables must be tucked away nicely inside the pile so no one can see. And then I must hurriedly get on the table and cover my lap with the paper table cloth like they said and smooth my hair and steady my breath so I appear once again to be in complete control, as if I wasn't terrified that door was going to open 30 seconds too soon, and the doctor and everyone in the hall would get a view of my full moon as I'm bent over trying to untangle myself from my pants. All this panic and madness so I can knowingly and purposefully hop up on the table, naked as a jaybird under a Scott towel so this doctor (or so they say) can come in (invited mind you) and examine my everything.

It's the same story every year. I'm just older each time and more aware that things aren't necessarily where they were the year before. This part of the appointment already preempted and damaged by the fact that before they can put me through this annihilation, they must WEIGH me first.

This year's appointment fell on June 23. The race completed, the gown adorned, the underwear hidden, the doctor entered the room. Let me say, I really like my gynecologist. I've had two gynecologists in my life and both have been fabulous. The first was a man. He delivered both my children, and I always knew I was in wonderful hands. The doctor I see now is a woman, and I find I have just as much confidence in her. And she's "close" to my age, and she's a girl so I know we have the same parts which is a plus.

The examination always begins with the breast exam. Lay back; please raise your arm above your head. They open your gown and rub your chest, and everyone pretends this isn't weird or awkward. She began with the right breast. There was small talk. I went to my happy place. And then she said, "You've got something here."

I said, "Huh?"

She said, "You have a cyst or something here. That wasn't here last year."

My response was, "Oh that reminds me. I was going to have you check a spot over here," and I touched my left side. Anybody else probably would have just gone silent and held their breath until she said, " *Oh, nope, never mind, it's nothing.*"

But not me. I must have been attempting the art of distraction. *"Hey, look over there!"*

She said, "It's probably a bone," and she felt the area on my left side I had pointed to. "Um, yeah, that's your rib," and she went back to the area she was more concerned about on the right. Still trying avoidance, I let my thoughts wander. Was I feeling smug because I'm thin enough that I confused a concerning area in my breast with a BONE or was I embarrassed that my chest is so small that you can FEEL bone? All the while she's still rubbing and pressing that one area, and I kind of just wanted her to stop it. Finally for lack of knowing what was expected of me at that moment, my left hand came up in slow motion and she took it and placed it on what she was feeling.

It was a lump. A definite, round ball-shaped lump. "How did I miss that?" I asked.

"I don't know," she said, "but I'm going to make you an appointment for a mammogram and an ultrasound. I'm sure it's just a fluid-filled cyst, but it's best just to make sure."

My mind was reeling. She completed the exam and moved on to Part 2. As she began the examination in my nether regions, I came around enough to say again, "No, really, how did I miss that?" What? Was I Rain Man all of a sudden?

I left that day with an appointment for a mammogram and an ultrasound scheduled for the following Tuesday. I was a bit in a fog, but realistically, how many times have I or someone else I knew had this very moment happen, and it's scary and then it turns out to be nothing. So I filed it away in the 'I can talk about it but not think about it file' and moved on.

The day after the mammogram and ultrasound (which I did not enjoy), I received a call that I needed a biopsy. The mammogram and ultrasound reports both stated the findings to be suspicious and a biopsy was required. I placed this in the 'file' and although it was on my mind, I was just ready to get it over with.

The biopsy was scheduled for July 14. It was an ultrasound guided needle biopsy. While watching through ultrasound, they numbed me, and then by using a needle with some sort of trigger, they were able to core the lump like an apple and take a sample. Super disturbing to think about, but for me completely painless. And the people that did the biopsy were so precious. At this point, my thought process was, "Man, I'm glad this part is over, and I'll just be glad for them to call or for me to get the letter in the mail that says in not so many words "Hey, everything is fine. Sorry you've wasted so much time worrying and now you have all these bills to pay for no reason."

But that's not how it happened.

The next day I received a call from the surgeon's office that did the biopsy.

"Hello! How are you?" I cheerily asked the nurse practitioner I'd seen the day before.

"Oh, today hasn't been a very good day," she said.

"I'm so sorry to hear that."

"Well, I'm afraid I'm not going to make your day very good either."

"Oh. Ok," I said quietly. Now the Becky in me still wanted to be cheery and distract her and avoid whatever it was she was about to say. But I waited.

"We got your pathology results back and it's cancer."

Our conversation continued, but I'm not exactly sure how I did that. I was smart enough to grab a pen and paper and just write down everything she said because although I was somehow asking questions, I was all the while almost having an out of body experience. It seemed like I was there, but I was simply listening to myself speak while that word just repeated over and over and over. Cancer, cancer, cancer, cancer, cancer.

Well, that's ridiculous. I literally thought of things that I only thought people said in movies. This happens to other people. This stuff doesn't happen to me. There's just been a mistake.

But it did happen to me, and there was no mistake.

I have breast cancer. Non-invasive ductal carcinoma and invasive ductal carcinoma.

Cancer. Never did I think that word would be associated with me. I couldn't even say it. I referred to it as "the ugly c-word."

August 2, with family and friends in the waiting room, I had a lumpectomy and had two lymph nodes removed. I now have two lovely scars. One under my arm that is about an inch to an inch and a half and one on my breast that is about 3 inches long. They actually don't bother me. I think of them as battle scars maybe. A physical proof that serves as a reminder when I think "This is NOT happening." Those scars say, "Oh yes it is." But I refuse to be ashamed of them. They are part of my story now, and I'll carry them with pride.

I suppose I'm a fast healer. Maybe I'm just stubborn. Maybe I just had a super duper surgeon. Any way you go, I did very well with the surgery.

So here we are, back at the present. We met with the oncologist on August 20, and we should be receiving the call this week stating whether I'll need 12 weeks of chemo or 20 weeks. So I'd say I'm chemo-bound within the next two weeks.

I wish I just knew when so I could plan. But for now, after a whirlwind, I'm spending my days close to my phone waiting for the call. Trying my best to prepare as best as I can for a temporary new life that's coming that I can't even really predict.

So this is where this journey has led me so far. Just writing all that was exhausting, but I'm glad I have it put into words. And now that I've started, I see I still have so much to say. But how much could this poor book actually hold?

How do I feel about it all? I think that's an important part of this self-counseling session I'm doing. So Becky, how are you feeling about all of this?

Well, I'm anxious about what chemo will be like. Will I be sick? What kind of fatigue are they referring to? Benadryl tired? Tired like I was at work the day after staying up all night waiting for my friend to have her baby? Or tired like I can't move my arms and legs and can't get out of bed or walk. I'm frightened about what is to come. I feel alone in a sea of people. I am devastated. I feel guilty for being so vain about losing my hair. I feel proud that I'm fighting a battle I'm going to win. I feel grateful for more things than I could ever write down.

I feel blessed.

Chapter 2

Baby steps...

For those of you that know me, I've always had either super long hair or longer than shoulder length hair anyway. At my 10-year class reunion, I know it sat above my shoulders, and that hair-cut was an accident. One of those times when you go to get a couple inches cut off, and they must have had some foreign kind of ruler. Anyway, I look back and it was cute but not me. Am I defined by my hair? I didn't really think so. I think I was wrong.

I tried to get the oncologist to tell me I was not going to lose my hair. He did not cooperate. I said, "Now, I have really THICK hair. So don't you think it'll just thin out some?" He still did not cooperate. No. I am going to lose all my hair. Generally, it happens two weeks after the first treatment and will begin to come back about six weeks after my last one. He and the fellow doctor in the room then told me that I will wake up one morning and my hair will be on my pillow and what's left will come out in handfuls. Can you say traumatizing? Jeez Louise. Is this whole thing not enough already that I'm going to be bald too? If I was just going to be sick or fatigued, I could stay home until I felt well enough to get out and about and put on my happy face, and maybe put it behind me for an hour or two or a day or two, however long I'm going to have that window of wellness before the next treatment sucks me under again. But how can I put it away for a bit and pretend like it's not happening when the proof is...well...on my head?

And what is that going to do to my babies? They go to bed one night and mom tucks them in and kisses their forehead, assuring them maybe even just with my presence and my smile that everything is going to be ok, and the next day after school they come home to a sickly, bald stranger. Actually that might be easier. Most likely they're going to be here when I wake up and mom is falling apart emotionally and physically.

And what about my husband? What is it going to do to him to see that happening to me and to see me broken more than maybe I already am? In one of the one million and one long and deep talks my husband, Kelley, and I have had, this time me trying to explain my fear of my hair loss, he said just the right thing.

"Baby, if you want a $1000 wig, I'll buy you a $1000 wig. If you want to go Kojak, you put your arm in mine and we'll walk down the street." I'll never forget that.

But I want to make it easy. I'm a fixer. I'm proactive. How can I make this go smoother for all of us?

So I started my *Baby Steps to Bald* project. Each week or so I'll go and get my hair cut a little shorter. There are short hair cuts I've always wanted to try and never would have been brave enough for. So last week I went and got the first hair cut of my program.

I had my friend, Heather, take my picture before she cut my hair and then after. I told her please not to worry if I cried. I'm a bit emotional these days. But the end result was great! I loved it. There were no tears. I took Kelley a little cutting of my hair. He had asked for a lock of it. When he saw me for the first time I was hoping for something like, "Dang woman! You look seeexxxyyyy!" But instead, his face lit up, and he smiled so big and said, "I love it. It looks so great! You look cute as a little bug!"

My son, Ryan, accepted it easily and my daughter, Mallory, adored it. In fact, she wants hers cut just the same.

It's strange though. It's a cute hair cut. It seems to suit me. It's just that, it doesn't FEEL like me. And I'll admit...these pictures make me cry. And that's ok.

Next week, maybe, on to hair cut number two. Stay tuned.

Chapter 3

Red hot mess, but I'm workin' on it...

Along with my chemo treatments coming up, they are also going to have to shut down my ovaries so I'll stop producing estrogen because my cancer is estrogen fed. Do you get it yet? They're going to put me into menopause. Good grief. It kind of makes me want to stick a fork in my eye. Actually, once the hot flashes and mood swings start, *Kelley* may want to stick a fork in my eye. What's that going to be like? (Not the fork in the eye...I'm talking about the menopause.) I'm already a red hot mess. I have never been so emotional in my life. When you realize that you cry during every episode of "Glee," you know something just ain't right. I make sure not to watch "Extreme Home Makeover". I wouldn't get out of bed the next day.

And then, BAM! I'm cleansed and bounce back to Beck in about 1.2 seconds. I think I might need to get my own place until this is over with.

My emotional state suffered Thursday at work when I made ANOTHER phone call to the doctor to ask about the results that should have already been in and the nurse told me that LAST Friday they had found out the tissue sample they sent on August 20 wasn't big enough for them to test.

I fell apart. I threw in the towel. I waved the white flag. I went home. I called Kelley and he dropped everything and came home himself and took over. I handed him the reins and let him handle it, and I did the Beck Bounce and watched some TV, resigned to whatever was going to happen. Just make them tell me something. Anything. Tell me the doctor is going to call me Tuesday at whatever time and then

ACTUALLY call me. Tell me that they've sent off another sample, and it'll be in next week or the next. Tell me they expect that I'll start treatment on a specific date. Just something.

Each day that passes that they haven't called allows a few more thoughts to creep in that I've been refusing so far. The whole point of me doing chemo even though the surgery was successful is that if there are cancer cells still in my body, they are microscopic and couldn't be detected yet. So the chemo is to kill all those bad boys. And if the cancer is estrogen fed and I'm still producing it at this very moment, then what if they're in there somewhere having a big old party, having a good time and multiplying. I don't WANT to do chemo. I'd like to stomp my foot and pout and say, "I don't wanna!" But then again, I'm terrified that I haven't started it yet.

But within 2 or 3 hours, Kelley had managed to get the doctor to call him back even though he wasn't at his office at Barnes that day. I didn't want to hear anything they said so I just kept on watching TV. Maybe ten minutes later he came in and said, "You start chemo next Friday."

I felt like one of those cartoon characters whose eyes were bugging out of their heads and I almost said in a panic, "Whoa there Bucko! What's the hurry?" Now after my emotional state taking a steady nose dive because I've been left hanging for 3 weeks, I'm freaking out because IT'S TIME!

I have my wits about me now though. Relief has set in because now we have a date. They still don't have the results, but the doctor is uncomfortable waiting much longer to start the treatments. So I'll do my first one this Friday and once the results come in, he will be able to determine whether I need to come two or three weeks later. If the results of the test come in that the cancer is low risk, I will do 12 weeks of chemo which will be one treatment every three weeks. If it comes back high risk, they'll want to do 20 weeks which will be a treatment every two weeks for the first eight and then once a week for the last 12. The doctor is kind of on the fence about it because if he was going by the size of the tumor, he would suggest the 12 because it was small. But because of my young age (which I love to hear) and because during surgery they found the cancer had begun to spread although it hadn't gotten to the lymph nodes yet, then that makes him prefer 20. So that's why he'd like to get these results before choosing a definite plan.

So now I have a start date! Great! Now what am I supposed to do with that? I have this panicked desire to PREPARE! Prepare what? I don't know. I need to get the house clean. I need to make lists and directions. I need to organize our bills so Kelley can get everything paid on time each month if I'm not feeling like helping. I feel like I need to go and do and be while I can. I feel like I need to cram an entire life into less than a week. A bucket list of sorts. I know I'm not dying. The chemo will not be the death of me. But in a sense, I feel like that first drop of chemo is going to mark the end of THIS Beck. This blonde-haired, healthy, goofy, giddy Beck.

Is her part in the story done? Will the chemo change who I am so much that when all the treatments (the chemo and radiation) are finished, I'm even unrecognizable on the inside? And how long is this part of the story going to go on? Six months? Eight months? A year? Do I need to Christmas shop this week in case I don't feel up to it in December? What about Mal's Halloween costume? Should I buy one now? Should I go sky diving or cliff jumping or ride the Amtrak somewhere just to say I did it? Will I have regrets no matter what I do these few days I have left before they start shooting poison into my body and change my life as I know it?

I don't know. I just don't know.

But what I do know is this. I have babies I'm going to see get married. I have grandchildren who I'm going to see graduate. I have great-grandchildren whose first cries I'm going to hear. I have a story to tell, and it sure doesn't end on

Friday. I'm stronger than cancer, and I'm sure enough stronger than chemo.

So bring it on.

Chapter 4

Movin' mountains...

Two months have crept and sped by all at the same time. July introduced us to breast cancer. August held my hand through the surgery that removed it from my body. Now September holds the starter pistol that begins the race to get my life back, that I know in my heart already will never be the same.

Chemo treatment number one is done. At 8:15 this morning, we had to get my base line labs done and then meet with the doctor to discuss "the plan." I feel like it's some secret op. at this point because we say that so much. I was totally ready for today. And yet, I cried as I sat in the main waiting room, surrounded by people with no hair who are already fighting their battle, realizing I really am one of them. A poignant moment I'd say, for me and possibly even for them if they happened to be looking my way. I just bet they felt this way too their first treatment and maybe even seeing my tears made them stand a little taller today, recognizing my position in this journey and remembering their own fears and emotions and seeing just how far in their battle they have come already. Today I was the newbie. But how can you sit in that room and look around and NOT gather strength from those amazing people? Some in wheel chairs, some wearing a mask, some as bald as could be and some with a wig or a do-rag. But ALL of them simply...people...waiting in a waiting room, just living their lives. I pictured some of them tapping their foot thinking, "Come on. Hurry up! If they'd just call me back, I could get back to work before the end of the day!" I'm glad my first day is over so now I can tap MY foot.

The results still aren't in. I don't even care about those dumb results anymore. They stress me out. I'm over them. I'll be doing the 20 week treatment plan. I'll have one treatment every two weeks the first eight weeks and then the last 12 treatments will be once a week. If the results EVER come in, and they scream that I don't need the 20, then if we feel it's best, we can modify it down to the 12 week. With the 20 week, I also have to have a shot the day after chemo to give my bone marrow a boost I think so I'm staying here at the hotel another night. If insurance will cover it, then either Kelley or I will do the next shots at home. Kelley's always asking me to play doctor with him and I keep saying no, so he's pretty excited. KIDDING! But that's funny.

Anyway, we were so excited to just finally KNOW the time frame of treatments that after the nurse and doctor left the room, Kelley and I literally high fived each other. "High five, Mama!" he said, "We've finally got us a plan!"

I changed out of the hospital gown (note...NOT a paper towel), and we sat and talked for a bit about things that were said and then I said, "Hey, wait, aren't we supposed to be somewhere?"

Kel said, "Shoot! Yeah, we were supposed to go to the treatment center across the hall!" So we'd been sitting in there like a couple of goobers, talking about how happy we were that we finally knew when I was going to start and for how long, which was NOW and we forgot to go. Sheesh.

Across the "hall" we went to the treatment center and signed in for chemo. I was asked again what town I lived in. Call me slow, but I finally understood today what that was all about. The receptionist said, "Where are you from?" I assumed it was for paperwork though.

"Bernie. It's a little bitty town in the Bootheel. About three hours away," I said.

"Well, I knew you weren't from around here with your accent."

Ohhhhhhhhhhh. I forgot that up here. WE are the ones with the accent, not the other way around. I'd found myself noticing each time how they talk so differently here when they're really not THAT far away. Then today I realized, "Holy Moly. I bet we've had them all twisted up in the game!" Like the time the doctor told me I would GAIN weight with chemo and I blurted out incredulously, "Well, I'm gonna be a big old tub o' lard!!!!" I wasn't doing that for comic relief. It just came out, and I'll never forget the blank look on his face or the fact that I guess I rendered him speechless.

But with the receptionist, the best part was when I tried to explain the size of our town.

"How big is Bernie?"

"Around 2000 people," I said.

"2000? Really?" she replied, her eyes wide.

"Yeah and we probably know most of them!" I giggled. "We're small enough we don't even have a McDonalds."

"NO MCDONALDS? Where do you eat then? Do you have to cook at home EVERY night?" she asked, astonished.

"Well, there's a McDonalds in the next town over, and we have little restaurants in town like Bernie Express."

"Oh is that like a little sub shop?" I could almost hear the relief in her voice.

"Ummmmm, no. It's more like going into someone's kitchen and telling them what you want to eat, and they fix it and you pay them."

"Oh, like Mel's Diner!!" she said.

"Um, nope, that's not it either." I almost explained the menu and considered telling her about Little House Restaurant too. I'm sure the name would have painted a picture in her mind of us loading up the wagon and grabbing our bonnets and headin' on down, but I didn't have the energy to explain. And frankly, all this restaurant talk of home was making me hungry for a country fried steak sandwich, and I had chemo to do so I sat down. I miss Mayberry.

I told Kelley, "We make friends wherever we go!" Today I made a new friend named Joy, one named Katie and Rhonda and lots that I suspect I'll see again but just don't know their names yet.

Katie took me on a tour of the treatment area. I was put in Pod 4. I like to say Pod. It sounds so Star Trek-y. It's just a room where there are two recliners, two beds and two chairs called the "Fast Track." That's for if you just need a shot or something that doesn't take long. I'll give the Fast Track a whirl in the morning when I go for my shot. Then next time I'll be in a private room. I'm going to have to have a port put in. Vanity is rearing its ugly head, and I just don't want ANOTHER scar on the other side of my chest. I just want to say, "Would you QUIT pickin' on me?" But the port will be a blessing. The chemo is tough on your veins, and the port just makes it so much easier. That's a small surgical procedure that they'll do right before my next treatment.

The treatment itself was fairly quick compared to what I expected. The nurse put the IV in and began the anti-nausea meds. Of course, going to the bathroom, which I had to do immediately because that's how I roll, is interesting. I have to unplug the IV stand and wheel myself through the room, around the other patients and nurses, and I'm a bit of a reckless driver with that thing.

Let me add that I love to get free stuff. Give me a free pen or pencil or pad of paper and I'm beside myself. That bag of goodies when I was pregnant with my kids (coupons, free sample of Dreft and Desitin), I might as well have just gone trick or treating, because I dumped those bags out in the middle of the floor and I "played" with each thing. So imagine my delight, when a nurse showed up with a TOTE BAG full of reading material and a little stress ball shaped liked a star! SCORE! This woman also stayed and gave me a binder to keep information in and then showed me a power point presentation on chemo and how it affects you.

As she's showing me the slideshow, my other nurse

came in to actually give me the chemo. It looks like Kool-Aid. Red Kool-Aid. And that makes you pee pink for a bit and that's cool. The Kool-Aid came in two big syringes and as she was slowly pushing it in, my eyes started burning a bit. Shoot! I was supposed to be paying attention to what she was saying! I'm sure it had to be important. I rubbed my eye. It still wanted to close. I grabbed the other eyelid and held it open. They just needed to shut for a second. Get it together, Beck! My arm itched a bit by where I was getting the chemo in the IV. I scratched it. My other arm itched. My cheek itched. My temple itched on the other side. My jawbone. What the poo? But no one seemed to notice my spastic behavior. Once the presentation was over, I raced my new wheels to the bathroom for a break and was greeted in the mirror by my face and neck decorated with red whelps. Really? Whatever. I rolled back out and stopped by the nurse, unphased at this point in the game.

"Um, yeah, so I think I've got something weird going on here," and I pointed to my face and neck.

"You're having an allergic reaction to something. I'll call the doctor. Are you having any shortness of breath?" she asked.

"No, I'm fine. Doesn't even itch anymore!" and I rolled on past. Small potatoes.

She came in and doped me up with some Benadryl. Which explains why I look drugged in this picture I had Kelley take. Because I was.

This.......is Beck on drugs. Any questions?

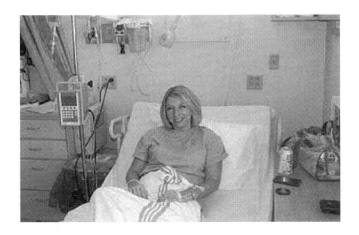

A friend of mine, Tracy, sent me a little book by Keith and Megan Provance called "Scriptural Confessions for Healing". The last couple of days have been tough, wrestling with the unknown, and I'm grateful for these words when I couldn't find my own.

'Speak to the Mountain'

--My words have power. Jesus said if I would speak to a mountain in my life and tell it to be plucked up and thrown into the sea it would have to obey me. So because Jesus said to do it, and because I am obedient to HIS commands, I speak to the mountain of sickness in my life.

Sickness, listen up, pay attention. I am talking to you! In the name of Jesus Christ, the Anointed one, I command you to be plucked up and thrown out of my life and body. You have no choice. You can't stay. You have to leave. There is no alternative, no other options. Pack your bags, hit the road, and don't come back anymore. Today's mountain is tomorrow's testimony. It doesn't matter how big the mountain is, and it doesn't matter how long the mountain has been there. What does matter is what Jesus says about the mountain. He said if I speak to the mountain, it has to obey me. My life is mountain free -- no mountains of sickness and disease here. The mountain of sickness has been eradicated and eliminated from my life. I am healed, healthy, and whole in Jesus' name. --

I'm speaking to my mountain!!! Can't wait to see it

move!!!

For tonight, over and out.

Chapter 5

Captain's log...

I remember taking the kids to the park one day and looking at the swings and thinking, *"You know what? I don't need anyone to push me and get me going these days. My legs are long, and I can touch the ground and they have power. I bet I could swing as big and high as I ever wanted now!"* So here I went with a mental skip and a hop and settled my hiney into one of those rubber seats of wonder and shoved off like nobody's business. Immediately, I caught air, and I pumped my legs again and again and I flew toward the sky, the wind blowing my hair back and rushing across my face. Higher and higher I went. I was so FREE! It was exhilarating! It was ....nauseating! Holy Moly! By the time I realized I had made a terrible mistake, I was zooming at about Mach 5 and had to ride it out until I slowed down enough to drunkenly flop off my perch and stumble toward a cool clump of grass under a tree where I gave myself a time out.

So that's not quite what I had expected. Life isn't always what we expect no matter how hard we try to plan and predict. And I definitely tried to plan and predict chemo.

I missed my son in the parade last night. Although as a junior high student, he's not playing his instrument this year. The fact that his hands hold one side of the banner that announces who that blue and white power band is coming down the lane has lost no significance on me. So as he donned his white shoes and snappy hat last night, I was lying in bed, and it hurt to miss it.

I giggle as I sit here because I found a note on my iPhone this morning that is dated this past Friday that simply says "4:40............Weird all of a sudden." I do NOT recall typing that and only found it because I needed to make a list of things we needed at Wal-Mart but for whatever reason I guess in the hotel room after treatment, I felt that MIGHT be pertinent information at some point in this whole chemo extravaganza. It's like I was starting my own little "Captain's Log," and I do NOT watch Star Trek, and frankly, I'm tired of making references to it so I need to stop. It only would have been funnier had I used the voice recorder on my phone to make it instead of the little legal pad application, with a whispery voice saying "4:40..........Feeling weird all of a sudden. I can't taste my soup and my hair feels funny."

I will also admit that on Friday, after the chemo Kool-Aid had been shoved into the IV, the hives had begun and the Benadryl had been administered, before I ever even got up off that bed and while I thought no one was looking, I gave my hair a little tug just to see if my body worked faster than the predictions of modern medicine and my hair was already loosening up. It was fine. And as of today, I still have my hair.

But although temporarily schizophrenic on Friday, I did well, and when Saturday morning rolled around, we made our way down to get my shot and then headed home. Although I think I kind of surprised us both when I climbed in the back of the truck right away but I had some episodes of "Glee" to watch and so I snuggled in. I didn't see a lot of anything except the back of my eyelids but by Cape Girardeau I was ready for a stroll through Sam's. Already things didn't taste good or, well, taste AT ALL so I wanted to try to get some soft peppermints that I knew I could buy in a big tub there, and I figured the walk would do me good. I was tired by the end of the venture but so far so good, and we set sail toward B-town.

And then I kind of can't remember Sunday. Not that I was doped up or anything. I just think it was uneventful and I felt tired and that was about the size of it, other than me thinking incorrectly that I was obviously at this point going to be unaffected by chemo.

Kelley's alarm went off Monday morning, and I got up and woke up the kids. Clothes picked out, teeth and hair brushed, PE clothes, lunch money for Mal, lunch box filled for Ry. I stood in the doorway and waved as they drove away and by the time Kelley got home from the seven minute trip, I was back in bed.

My body was so heavy. My bones ached from the shot and from being in bed for so long. I didn't like Monday, and I guess have blocked much of it out which is why my words about it are sparing. In a nut shell though, I think it was the worst day so far.

Yesterday morning after the alarm, I made it a whole two hours maybe and although I didn't hurt as bad or feel as heavy, my eyes literally refused to stay open for most of the day. And even though I missed the parade last night, I did get to have a little picnic with Mal sitting on my bed, talking about her day and tales of her own fourth grade nothing.

So, after Monday being so rough and Tuesday being so weak, I predicted today to be "All Day Awesome!" But this morning I got out of bed and couldn't get my kids ready for school. I just couldn't do it. I gave birth twice with no pain medication, and today I couldn't even muster up the energy to wake them up and simply encourage them to get dressed and then go make them a sandwich. Kelley stepped in of course and got them ready for their day, and I lay on the couch. I had started some coffee first thing, and I guess maybe it finally settled in and about 8:30 or so, I talked myself into a shower.

Maybe I needed to get out. I hadn't been out of the house since Saturday, and I thought that would do me a world of good. And suddenly, a bacon, egg and cheese biscuit sounded great. So I put my makeup on and fixed my hair for the first time since Saturday, ready for Hardees and a stroll through Wal-Mart. But by the time I got ready, I was so worn out I didn't think I was going to be able to go. I climbed in the truck and by the time we got to the bank to run through the drive thru, I was literally wiped out.

And I felt ashamed. I couldn't hold my head up, and I was embarrassed. All I could think of was "I'm failing." I'm supposed to be fighting this and instead I'm so weak I can barely get myself together four full days later. But although tears are readily available these days, I fought the urge to bawl all the way to Malden. And I ate my biscuit, and I tooled around Wal-Mart and climbed into bed when I got home.

I didn't expect this to be fun. I didn't expect this to be easy. But I was going to be tough. Never let 'em see you sweat! I can bring home the bacon.......fry it up in a pan! Well, jeez, there isn't a bit of either one of those statements that makes any sense or amounts to a hill of beans. I think I've misconstrued the meaning of "fight." I said I was strong! I said I'm a fighter! I said I'm going to beat this cancer and chemo isn't going to get the best of me. But I realized today, fighting isn't battling unscathed. The dictionary says that fighting means to make a strenuous or labored effort. Well, sheesh, I'm doing that!

I guess what I'm trying to say is, sometimes you just have to reevaluate. Look at those expectations again and say, "Now, where was I going with that?"

I've got about 15 chemo treatments left. But you know what? I've got one already done! And maybe I can't hold my head up, but the bright side is getting to take as many Big Fat Guilt-Free Medicated OR Non-medicated naps as I want!!!!!!

So today's deep thought...........If the swings make me hurl, I'll just go down the slide.

Chapter 6

It's time...

Waiting for your hair to fall out is kind of like expecting a baby. Is it time? Is that a contraction or just gas? Did my scalp just tingle for no reason or was that a hair follicle sliding out of place? Is my bag packed? Is it time for my last hair cut yet? Should we call the doctor? Should I call my hair stylist? Did my water just break? Can I pull out a handful yet?

Every day I say to Kelley, "I think my hair feels loose today." It's freaking me out. As a kid, when I lost a tooth, it was the most natural thing in the world. I just went on about my day and enjoyed sticking a piece of corn where my tooth was before or being able to drink through a straw with my teeth closed together. But losing a tooth as an adult is not natural. My hair falling out is NOT natural.

Like I'm watching a scary part of a movie through my fingers, each morning I lift my head and look with one eye closed at my pillow to see if my hair came out while I was sleeping. This morning was no different and my pillow was clean, hair still intact.

I got the kids up and ready for school and as I walked past Ryan's mirror, I noticed one hair sticking straight up on top of my head. As lazy as it sounds, if I've ever had a hair out of place, rather than stress about it, I'd just yank it out. One little sting and then the bad hair part of my day was over. So this morning when that hair caught my attention, I just took hold of it and gave it a yank. And it just came out. There was no sting, no element of discomfort. Just........pfffffffff. If my hair made a noise coming out, that would be it.

I stood for a minute and glared at the hair in my hand. "Kel," I said. "I just pulled out a hair that was sticking up and it didn't put up a fight."

He made a face like, "Uh oh," and we just kind of stood there for a second.

And all I could think of was "It's time. It's happening. This is it. What do I do?" See, labor mentality tells you to start timing contractions. Since it was my hair loosening its grip, I felt like I needed to make a chart and keep track of how many hairs I lost each hour throughout the day so I'll know how close I really am to BALD.

Instead, I made a hair appointment. Ten HUT! Straighten up, Soldier! There's a program in place here, and it's time for step two.

So at 12:30 today, as part of Beck's Baby Steps to Bald project, I got my second hair cut. Last week I don't think I was ready. But today I was. Kelley was with me this time and took pictures for me. Heather cut the back first which was probably the scariest part but when she started on the front, Kelley said, "Is this hair cut going to make her sassier? Because she's already starting to look sassy to me." That might be code for, "She's been a real pain in the toot for about a week and a half." But he says he likes it and has told me repeatedly today that when this is all over with I should do it like this again. All amazing words from a man who I think was as comforted by my long hair as I was.

I didn't cry about the haircut. I had already accepted it and even took a phone call from the insurance company about my shots while she finished.

Later though, as Kelley and I stood together in front of the mirror, where moments before I had easily pulled a few more strands out of my brand new hair cut, my heart broke a little.

This is part of the journey. It's time. And I'll welcome these tears to wash this moment away and smooth the path til the next chapter.

Chapter 7

Rest through my winter...

As we drove to St. Louis Thursday, I noticed the leaves are beginning to turn on the trees. October is here and fall is upon us. Like a Bob Ross painting, I imagine happy little squirrels gathering nuts and stockpiling for winter. Soon the trees will be a myriad of golds and reds and oranges, glowing like the flames of a bonfire. Thoughts of s'mores and hayrides warm my insides. But before long, winter will beckon to those leaves to loosen their hold from the limbs they hang from.....just as my head is loosening its hold on my hair.

Thursday we packed our things and took off to St. Louis. Of course, I wanted to stop in Cape. We decided to eat at McAllister's first. It's our favorite place to eat, and Kelley loves to order the Big Nasty because it sounds like something he shouldn't say. As we sat down, I ended up seated with my back to the window.

After a bit, Kelley's eyes got a little wider and he said "You're hair is very........."

"What? Is it falling out right now?" I asked.

He shook his head slightly and said, "With the window behind you and the light shining in, you can see that you have strands of hair just not connected, and they're standing up all over and hanging out the bottom."

All I could say was, "Please Lord, just let it hang on until we get to St. Louis."

And when Kelley decided to order a scrumptious slice of Key Lime Pie that he shared with me, and the bite I took made me shudder and shake my head, he just looked at my hair and said, "Don't do that." As if any move, any shimmy was going to set my hair into a domino effect, and I might begin to molt right there in the restaurant. And heaven forbid, WHAT IF I SNEEZED?

We left McAllister's and got to the mall and of course, as we walked in, a gust of wind blew up and wanted to tousle my hair like it was playing and saying, "Hey little Buddy, how ya been?" NOOOOO! Get your windy mits off my hair. The texture was even different. It didn't blow or flow or swing anymore. So that gust of friendly wind was a burr in my tail, and I put both hands on my head and raced into Barnes and Noble to the bathroom to pull out the new loosey goosies and put what was there back where it belonged and pick the rest off of my shirt.

After our trek through the mall and as we were heading back to Barnes and Noble to exit the mall and get right to the car, Kelley has a genius idea.

"Hey, you wanna go in the hurricane machine?" he said. Now the hurricane machine, if you don't already know, is a box in the middle of the mall that you can get in and experience what the winds from a hurricane might feel like while everyone watches.

So of course, I gave Kel the look that said, "No. Now go sit over there and think about what you just said."

Then he got a look like a bright light bulb had just gone off above his head. "Beck, no really! We could make a fortune! Your hair is coming out anyway but these people don't know that! I could draw a crowd and say I've souped up this machine so much that it could blow someone's hair right off their head. I could charge $5 a person to see if I could really make it happen and then YOU could volunteer! We'd be rich and your hair wouldn't be loose anymore!"

We left the mall without stepping into the hurricane machine but you've got to admit, that would have been hilarious.

My hair hung on until St. Louis. It was a trooper. I tried to make a game plan. How can I do this so it's the easiest? Kelley finally said in the truck when we were driving in to the Lou, "Listen, I'm just here. I want you to do this however feels the most comfortable for you. If you want to wash it, straighten it, curl it, smack it up, flip it, rub it down, oh nooooo, then that's your prerogative. And I know that was just a bunch of 80's songs lumped together, but what I'm saying is I'm right here ready to do whatever you need me to do whenever you are ready for me to do it."

So later in the hotel room, I showered and washed my hair for the last time. I still don't know why. And each handful of hair that came out I lay in a nice little pile so I could refer back to it at a glance when my mind tried to run away. I got dressed in my Hope t-shirt. I put my makeup on. I called Kelley in the bathroom........and I couldn't do it. I cried. I wailed. "I can't believe I'm having to do this. I don't understand this. It's too hard. I can't do this. How am I supposed to do this?" I said it over and over until I was washed clean of my hurt and dismay. He asked if I wanted to sit and I said "No, I'll stand." I grabbed the counter and closed my eyes and as he turned on the clippers and started carving out the new me, I simply prayed and gave thanks. I thanked God for this beautiful man who loves me enough to relieve me of my "crown and glory" when I wasn't strong enough to do it myself. I thanked God for His healing power. And then I opened my eyes. And do you know who stared back at me? ME! Peace poured out of me. Strength flowed through me. With each breath I was stronger. Each moment brought one less tear. And inside I sang the words to my newest theme song by India Arie. *I am not my hair. I am not this skin. I am the soul that lives within.*

And then I said, "Stop."

Kelley turned off the clippers and said, "What?"

I smiled and said, "I want a mohawk." And so we made me one. Maybe someday I'll share those pictures.

In the end, after two haircuts and three showers, I stood in the mirror and saw the woman standing before me was the same woman who about two hours earlier had been Kelley's wife of 15 years, the same woman who is the mother of Ryan and Mallory, the same woman who is the daughter and granddaughter of her parents and grandparents. Who knew that underneath all that hair was still me?

Then Kelley said, "Now we're going for a walk."

"Honey, I'm so tired and it's 12:30 a.m.," I said.

"Then this will be the perfect time for you to practice. There won't be many people out."

"I'm not really ready to go out like this," I confessed.

"Ok, that's fine," he said. "Then wear your Beau Beau or your wig. However you want to do it."

So I put on my pink Beau Beau scarf. We walked out of the hotel room, and I put my arm in his and we walked down the hall. And then we got on the elevator. And then we walked all around the parking garage and we talked and talked. And later when I said I might not be able to sleep because my head was cold, he said, "It won't be......because I'll hold it." And he placed his sweet hands on my head and kept me warm.

I didn't want to post pictures anywhere of my haircut until both of my children had seen it and were comfortable. When we got home and I saw Ryan for the first time, I was wearing my Beau Beau, which is a scarf I ordered on-line made by a design by a beautiful woman with alopecia. They are premade to fit the size of your head, come in all different materials and fun colors. When I offered to take it off, Ryan said "No, no, no." Although it surprised me a little, I hurt for him. And so we made a plan. When I need a minute or two without a covering on my head and need to feel bald and free, I'll go to the bedroom and lock the door and put up a sign that says Bandanna Off. He liked that plan. But Mallory busted in the house on me with Kelley, and I didn't get my door shut in time and she saw me. I apologized, but she was ok with it or seemed to be at least. Ryan has now seen a picture of my new do on my mom's phone of his own accord. Yet he's still not ready for the real deal. It's ok. We have time.

I can't help but think it was God's grace that allowed such a huge event in my life like my hair falling out to happen in the privacy of a hotel room, where Kelley and I could take our time and shed our tears and even laugh a little and then take that midnight stroll in my Beau Beau. And my children did not have to suffer through that. I am blessed. I see more and more evidence every day that God knows exactly what we need long, long before we do.

And so, like the changing seasons, as we watch summer turning to fall, and fall peacefully floating into a sleeping winter and awakening again in the spring, abundant in life and vibrant in color, I too will rest through my winter and wait patiently with an already thriving spirit for my own spring.

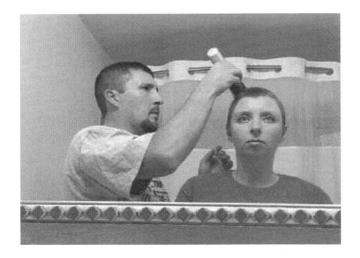

A brand new day...... GI JANE

The wig brings Good Old Beck back.

The Beau Beau

Chapter 8

One of those moments...

After a long emotional night, last Friday morning came and I'm not exactly sure how I was feeling. My hair was suddenly gone, and now I was scheduled for a port placement and round two of chemotherapy. That's a lot to digest in a short span of time.

The sun DID come up, however, just like any other day. The world didn't stop because I got a new hairdo. So I got up and got dressed and who would have thunk it, but without hair it takes me a LOT less time to get ready in the morning. We had time to spare! We lolly-gagged even. So we used our extra time to take a few pictures of my new do and begin to embrace the new me.

But considering at 7:55, when Kelley looked at our paperwork and realized I was supposed to have been there to get my labs done at 7:30 and that my port placement was scheduled for 8:00, well, it kind of stole my thunder.

"Dang it, Kel! This is NOT a drill! This is my first time really going out in public in the day time, and I don't even have my Beau Beau on right!" And we raced out the door.

Of course, we can't just be thirty minutes late. No. Everything also has to be on separate floors. We had to pick up my prescriptions and get my lab work done on the 7th floor. The port placement surgery itself scheduled at 8:00 was on the 3rd floor. That's not counting the appointment with my doctor afterward back on the 7th floor and then my chemo treatment scheduled after that. And the time now was about 8:03. Ahhhhhh!!!!! So Kelley sent me sailing to the 7th floor for labs while he ran to the 3rd floor to run interference. Then

I booked it back down the elevator, Beau Beau flopping in the breeze, just praying I'd put it on straight and that my newly buzzed head wasn't sticking out weird somehow to make people say, "Well, bless her heart." And on top of that, Kelley didn't have phone service so he didn't answer when I called, and I was racing around the 3rd floor aimlessly wondering where do me and my Beau Beau go?

But as if this was simply par for the course in the day to day goings on at Barnes or, even better, as if this day only revolved around me........thirty minutes late for labs? Don't worry. Fifteen minutes late for my port placement? No big deal. Do I ever plan to screw up like that again? Ummm.....no. Well, it's not my plan anyway.

Here we go again though with the "Here's your gown. Remove everything above your waist. Open in the front. Please remove your necklace."

But they didn't mention my scarf. So when they came back in the room, I just bit the bullet and said, "Ok, so I got this new haircut last night. Do you want me to take this scarf off?" They assured me it was fine to leave it on but after they wheeled me into the surgical room and I slid from gurney to table, the sweet nurse was concerned she might ruin my pretty pink head covering while prepping me for surgery. So I grabbed the bull by the horns and said, "Take it off. I'm ok." So in a twilight state of mind, Beck wore her big girl panties and bared her bald head for the first time.

Because the chemo they are giving me is so aggressive, it is very hard on my veins. Even this time, lab work and the IV for the twilight medication they gave me to get the port bruised me pretty badly. The port itself is a cylinder with a hollow space inside that is sealed by a soft top that makes me think of a rubber screen. It's connected to a small, flexible tube and when a special needle is put through the "screen, " it creates easier access to my bloodstream for the chemo or even blood work. Now an hour or so before labs or chemo, I have a cream or an ointment that I will put on to numb the area, and when I go to the lab or treatment center, I just check "port" on the chart now instead of "arm" and they'll be able to start access through there. No muss. No fuss. Well.........less muss........less fuss.

I was afraid that they would put it on the opposite side as my lumpectomy and have my chest even more scarred up than it already is, but I was blessed that they decided to do it all on one side. So now, I have two new scars added to my collection. One about an inch long that is an inch or two above my lumpectomy scar and a smaller one on my collar bone.

And let me say, I DO appreciate how much easier it is and how much easier it will be from here on out. But now I have this THING in my chest that I can see........I can feel. I need it to be incognito........invisible......because it just creeps me out and especially this close to Halloween. Seems like I see it or a version of it on every new scary movie trailer they show on TV.

Whining aside though........no wait. I'm not done. The anesthesia, the lovely twilight medication, that, while it's working, is a very pleasant experience, made me feel yucky after surgery. When I went for the dreaded weigh in and vitals before chemo, the nurse, Joy, said, "Are you ok?"

I said, "Yeah. Like my new hair cut?"

She said, "Well, I have to say you look beautiful," and I could hear the BUT coming so I knew she was sugar coating something. "But your demeanor just isn't the same," she said. Translation..........Yep, the hair cut is obvious, but you're acting weird too.

I just replied, "Yeah, I don't think that anesthesia made me feel very good."

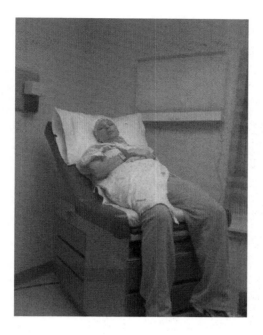

Soon though, in the doctor's office, I was able to lie down (after changing into my gown of course) and a little power nap set me straight. Then back out to the waiting room we went after getting our little Outback Steakhouse buzzer so we would know when it was our turn to go back for my chemo treatment.

And then the most amazing thing happened.

A bell.

Was it a fire? No, in a facility like this there would have been sirens and whistles and flashing lights. This was just the simple clang, clang of a bell. And I will never forget sitting in my seat with Kelley standing in front of me and noticing people in the waiting room beginning to applaud.

"She's done," Kel said, almost under his breath, as we watched a woman walking away from a bell hanging on the wall. I didn't understand. "With her chemo," he said. "She just rang the bell to celebrate her last treatment."

I was in awe. Tears were hard to hold back. What an

empowering moment to be able to share with a complete stranger. And don't you see? If we'd been on time that morning.......if we hadn't shown up 30 minutes late for labs........we would have missed it. God's grace again.

Before I left that day, I made sure I stopped by that bell and took a good look. And when I pictured the day that my children stand beside me and watch my own hand ring that bell, I definitely smiled.

"Life is not measured by the number of breaths we take, but by the moments that take our breath away. Smile.....this is one of those moments."

20 weeks of chemotherapy.....

16 treatments total.....

Chemo #2.............Complete.

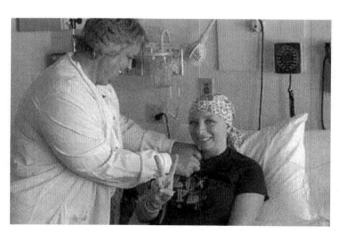

Chapter 9

This woman's work…

I suppose I've been dragging my feet about writing. I haven't had the energy to get my thoughts to paper. And in all honesty, I already knew that this entry most likely will not be one of my favorites. There probably won't be funny little anecdotes and stories to tell. I find I'd rather only write if I'm strong. I'd rather only tell the tale when I'm bigger than cancer and braver than chemo. I wish I could say that after having three treatments under my belt, that this is a piece of cake and that I am tougher than nails and am flying through this unscathed like a superhero with unbelievable powers and force fields.

But some days I am not strong.

And some days I am not brave.

Some days I am sad and discouraged.

And sometimes there are reasons.

And sometimes there just aren't.

I don't want to talk about this part of the story. The "Becky" in me knows if she waits long enough, just gives it a few more days maybe, that I'll forget these rough patches and be able to bask in the glory of the bright side of this whole mess. But I realize denying the real story isn't fair to me or anyone else for that matter. This is my therapy. This book has been good for me. I write my honest to goodness thoughts, and once I finish a chapter, I feel a little lighter. I think today I could stand to feel a little lighter. It's been a long and tough ten or so days, and it's time for a cleansing.

Two Thursdays ago, Mallory woke up super tired with a tummy ache. I made a mental note but chalked it up to the

"Thursday School Day Blues" and sent her on her way.

It wasn't long after that though that school called, and Kelley had to pick up a sick girl. Headache, vomiting, fever.

Days 7 - 10 after chemo for me are the days when my counts are the lowest, and I am the most susceptible to getting sick if someone around me is running a fever or has something I could catch. Day 7 for me was the next day.

So as if those red, round, flashing lights began to go off, and the alarm system began to sound -- BAH BAH BAH BAH--, the "metal gates" dropped down over mine and Mallory's doors and Kelley had us on lock down.

So there we were, mother and daughter, separated by a hallway...a world apart.

And she knew. Kelley said when she got home and was sick in the bathroom, she just kept saying she was sorry. "I'm sorry, Daddy. I'm sorry I'm sick. Mommy doesn't need to be around this." No! That's not the way it's supposed to be! Why should any 9-year old have to ever let a guilty feeling or thought pass through their precious mind over something like this?

Then when Kelley woke me up Friday night to say he thought he might need to take her to the ER because she was running a 105 degree temperature, well that was one of those moments that brought me to my knees. I needed to hold her and touch my lips to her forehead to see about her fever like mommies do. I needed to hold her hair back when she was sick and put a cool rag to her face.

But I couldn't get near her.

How could that possibly have made her feel? Only being able to hear mommy's voice on the other side of the door or only seeing me wear a mask from across the room, conscious and obviously ridden with guilt because a stupid virus or sickness of some kind that she carried, FAR from her fault, was keeping us separated.

These are the days that put chinks in my warrior armor.

And then there is the vanity aspect of this journey.

Although my hair falling out and having to make the choice to shave it was also one of the toughest things I've ever had to go through, I have to say, I miss my little buzz cut. Within days, the buzz wasn't short enough and as my hair continued to fall out, I felt and looked as though I had mange. So I had Kelley buzz it closer which ended up a bit like sandpaper. It worked nicely like Velcro though to keep my wigs and scarves from slipping. But that length, as odd as it sounds, was painful.

So once again, Kelley and I sat in the bathroom for over an hour while he played barber shop and shaved my head. Five razors later, my head shines like a diamond and is smooth as a baby's butt. And I can't seem to get past it. I realize now how much of a security blanket that little buzz cut was.

So as this journey progresses and chemo takes its toll physically and emotionally, it's things like these that, as much as I don't want to admit it, make me heavy laden and put me in my bed with thoughts of just staying there until this is over.

When will this be over?

But the last few days I've found myself thinking back to earlier this year when *American Idol* aired on TV, before cancer became part of my world. There was a contestant, Big Mike that sang a song by Maxwell called "This Woman's Work." I'd heard it before and liked it, but it was just the sound that touched me. The meaning of the song I didn't quite understand. So I looked up the lyrics and watched the actual videos on *YouTube* and once I understood it, for some reason I just couldn't get enough of it.

And now as I hear it, it means much more than it did when it was just a touching song about some man and some woman.

> *"Pray God you can cope, I'll stand outside*
> *This woman's work, this woman's world*
> *Ooh it's hard on the man, now his part is over*
> *Now starts the craft of the Father."*

I remember right after I was diagnosed, before surgery, before chemo, on a day when it was too much and my mental exhaustion sent me to bed for an un-Becky-like nap, I woke up to find Kelley kneeling beside the bed, just looking at me.

"What are you doing?" I asked.

"Just watching you sleep."

What can this be like for him? I saw the pain in his eyes when HE had to be the one to shave my head. And I saw his hurt days later when I finally understood that where I blamed the chemo for me losing my hair, he blamed himself. Knowing it was his own hand that did the work was too much for him, and even when it was too much...he did that for me anyway.

How selfish of me? How dare I even consider laying down until this is over when there is this man who is by my side every day, through every appointment, who takes charge of my medicine and gives me a shot every two weeks and is present to catch the words I don't hear from the doctor...watching me in a battle he can't fight for me.

How can I threaten, even simply in my own mind, to lie down until this is over, when my children can't. My children, whose lives have been just as turned upside down as mine, who are having to learn to cope themselves with this new life and with this "different" mom.

How can I even entertain the thought of just "waiting til it's over" when I have family and friends lifting me up with cards and messages and taking time from their own lives to do fundraisers for us and to bless us with meals during this difficult time so I can REST, not LAY DOWN.

Bare bones truth about chemo...honest to goodness truth...it's trying to wear me down. I've been waiting for a good day to write because I'd rather paint a pretty picture. But that's not the real story. The real story is the chemo makes me so tired and yet I can only sleep so much. It gave me mouth sores although that particular side effect has been manageable and although painful at the time, short-lived. Yesterday it became apparent that what I had joked about as "chemo brain" is beginning to set in after this treatment. The silly rattlings that just used to be Good Ole Beck now have a different meaning. I'm beginning to forget what I just said or what I was going to say or who I actually said that to. I'm beginning to have more trouble remembering words as I'm talking. Kelley was concerned enough to call my nurse yesterday to find out why this treatment has been harder on me physically than before and why I'm a little more scattered than usual. And the fact of the matter is, it's chemo and this is part of the game. The Neulasta shots that he has to give me make me hurt, and the super doses of steroids they have me on have made me gain weight.

And I hate it all.

But...my daughter is well now, and I can hug her and hold her all I want. And we were blessed by our wonderful friend, Cory, who took time from his own family that night to make an emergency house call and reassure us that all would be well.

And when Kelley had Mal in the tub that night to try to break her fever, and I could hear her sweet murmurs through the wall just loud enough to crush this mommy's heart, it was my son that climbed in bed with me and rested his hand on my arm and talked to me about everything under the sun until my tears subsided.

Sometimes I forget to look, but my glass is half full...not empty. I will REST when I'm tired. I will not give up. I will accept that some days will be hard and discouraging, but I will know that tomorrow will be brighter. I will remember that this isn't just about me and that there are others standing outside, depending on me to make it go away.

This woman's work is not done.

Chemo #3 - Check.

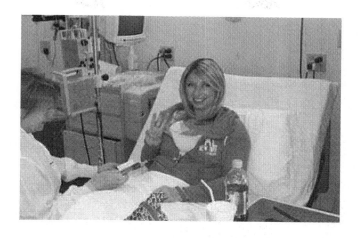

"*I consider that our present sufferings are not worth comparing with the glory that will be revealed in us.*" -- Romans 8:18

Chapter 10

Just chemo…

That's what Kelley caught me saying as we prepared to leave for my 3rd treatment. I was referring to the fact that that particular trip would probably be fairly easy considering there would be no lumpectomy, no port placement, and no surgery of any kind. I expected that time to be easier because it would be "just chemo." How strange to realize chemotherapy has become somewhat "old hat."

For whatever reason, the week after chemo #3 was the toughest yet, physically and emotionally. But the second week was brighter and lighter. Maybe it was just the beautiful October weather, but whatever it was, my energy level was up and I pushed myself a bit to get out and about, even though it was just to the post office or the Dollar Store. For me, those were giant leaps. But last week's energy boost, although wonderful during the day, continued on and resulted in a week of chemo insomnia. It's always something. Now that I understood the cycle though, I was confident that the insomnia would soon be replaced by plenty of sleep after the next treatment. I was right.

As routine though as chemo has become, this whole port access process before each treatment is really holding me back from being "one" with chemotherapy. The port access at chemo #3, my first actual access in the lab where I sat in the chair and they actually placed the needle in my chest, wasn't quite as easy as I had been led to believe. The port DOES make chemo easier. I guess we just never discussed what had to happen first. Just as I was the only one they'd ever seen to break out in hives during chemo, I'm not making this whole port thing easy either. I don't mean to be complicated. I'm just making things interesting I suppose.

As the nurse accessed the port for the first time and then wanted to use it for blood work immediately, I'm assuming usually a general procedure, things were complicated by the fact that as she tried to draw my blood, well, it didn't want to come out. Really? Since starting chemotherapy, a prick from a sticker burr from our over run yard begins an immediate and fairly steady flow of blood and yet when it matters, when I have a needle sticking out of my chest, my stubborn blood says "Um, no, I don't think so."

And as if just seeing this port in my chest every day isn't enough to give me the willies, having a nurse try to flush my port with a syringe full of fluid, pumping it like she's airing up a bicycle tire with no results, doesn't make me any calmer. Then knowing her request for me to take a deep breath, to cough, to now turn my head and then cough again, is actually me manipulating my veins to turn my proverbial "faucet" on so my blood begins to flow, well, that sure made me dread going back for another treatment.

Our friend and pastor, Jared, came to see us right before we left Thursday. As we visited, I revealed I was nervous about the whole port thing and that I was dreading the chance that I might have to play a part again in making things "flow smoothly" when it was time for lab work again. Before he left, he offered to pray with us, and he asked if there was anything specific I'd like him to pray about. I said peace. I just wanted to have a sense of peace about walking in to that lab and possibly having to go through another experience I definitely do not deem pleasant. I just didn't want to be anxious about the procedure I knew was looming the next morning.

And that was actually the perfect time for words he had just shared with us to fall into place.

"Therefore humble yourselves under the mighty hand of God, that he may exalt you in due time, casting ALL your care upon Him, for He cares for you." 1 Peter 5:3-7

So when I went in for the port access the next morning, she handed me a mask and donned one herself and said, "One, two, three" and jabbed that needle in my chest. And again when the blood didn't flow, I took heart and didn't panic. When the deep breaths and the coughs produced nothing, I had peace. And when in the end, I was upside down in the recliner on my head, turned on my left side with my right arm lifted, I just looked at Kelley and smiled.

And then there was "just chemo."

I am well. I am achy and sleepy. My eyes refuse to stay open for long and my body is too heavy at times to get off the couch or out of the bed for any length of time. But this is temporary Chemo #4 is complete, the final of my four aggressive treatments. I received my last Neulasta shot on Saturday. In two weeks, I will return for a new part of my journey, 12 more chemo treatments. These are once a week. I'm not sure what these hold in store for me, but I am sure glad to turn the page and start on a new chapter of my story.

Chemo #4 - Finished.

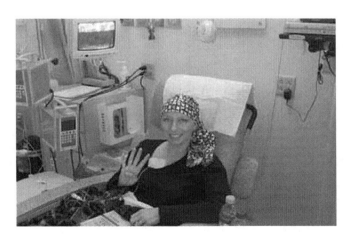

Chapter 11

Stripped...

I have heard my mom tell people about how many vacuum cleaners she went through over the years when I was younger because of all the abandoned Lee Press On nails she sucked up. I can also remember asking her if I could use our tape to make fingernails and then I would sit patiently for an hour ripping off 2 inch pieces of clear tape, sticking them to each of my nail beds and meticulously cutting the ends with scissors to a lovely pointed shape. Voila! My first set of "acrylics!" They lasted just long enough for me to get up and put away the tape and scissors, and then one or two would get stuck to the drawer I was closing and when I tried to get loose then two of the others would be stuck together and another would be folded backwards. The end result....a wad of tape and a lost hour or so but man had they looked good when I squinted!

If I really wanted to go WAY back, I can still remember my first bottle of nail polish. It was red and I believe it might have been made by Crayola. I would paint my nails just right and then because it had a rubbery nature, later in the day I could peel each one off in one piece.

I can even remember in high school, I once painted my nails and put a polka dot on each one. Then each day I added another dot of a different color just to see if anyone would notice. And they didn't.

Call it fascination. Call it destiny. Call it whatever you want. But you see, I was meant to be a nail technician. How else can you explain that 11 years after opening my shop, until breast cancer, I still couldn't wait to get to work every day?

Through a Google "accident," I came across some information that indicated this woman who was doing chemotherapy was wondering when she would lose her fingernails. EXCUSE MOI? Wow, she must have had some bad stuff! What kind of cancer could she possibly have had? Oh...breast cancer? Well, she must just be from somewhere far off like Duluth or something. People around here don't take chemo treatments and lose their fingernails. I know because I would have heard about it by now.

Just in case, I questioned a couple of people about it and then questioned my doctor's nurse on the phone one day. I explained to her that I am a nail tech, and I had on acrylics and that I was sure that was no problem but I wanted to check just to be sure that I could wear them during treatments.

"Well," she said, hesitantly, "the chemo could change your nails somewhat."

"So, you're saying I should take my acrylics off?" I asked.

"Yeah, probably so," and we just left it at that.

Well, kick me in the crotch. I just shook my head and started taking them off.

So there you have it. I suppose that's it then. The sun has not been tanning me too much through the windows of my home, and I have already almost graduated from pale to transparent. I am bald and my eyelashes are slowly making an exit, sure to be sped up soon by the new chemo I am starting tomorrow. And now possibly my fingernails? Talk about stripped. I'm going to be...naked! It's like that recurring dream people have of showing up at school and standing in the middle of the cafeteria, realizing too late you hurried too fast getting ready that morning and forgot to put clothes on and everyone is laughing and pointing and staring. Well, shoot. Now I bet I'm going to dream about that tonight.

And here's something I've learned about me. I can't work a wig. Before I lost my hair, there was a day I was going to be home alone all day and I decided it was the perfect opportunity to wear my blonde wig and get comfortable with it while piddling around the house. It did not go well. I remember finally calling my mom and saying, "This wig is dumb," and I retired it to its little plastic wig head stand for the day.

Two days later, home alone again, the challenge of the wig beckoned to me and I again pulled all of my own hair up in that little panty hose bald cap and gave the wig another whirl. And it looked pretty good! Now what difference did two days make that made it look right on Wednesday when it had been so wrong on Monday. Turns out I'd had it on crooked.

I wore my wig to St. Louis two treatments ago and as usual, once we arrived, we hit Applebee's downstairs in the hotel. Being my first time eating and wearing a wig, at some point in the meal, I ended up with more of the wig in my mouth than the bite of food I had taken. I can only hope no one saw that.

I wore it again the next day to my treatment. I am always scheduled to see the doctor before the actual chemo for a brief exam and to go over how I've felt this time around. I realized as they handed me the infamous gown that the wig was probably a bad idea. I worked hard to get that fake hair in place and brushed. Now I had to get my shirt over my head without messing my do. But with Kelley's help and thank goodness for that mirror on the back of the door, I was in place by the time the doctor came in. And then, so focused on the discussion with the doctor, I temporarily forgot about the (unattached mind you) quaff on my head and when he asked me to lie back on the table, I did so with a little too much gusto and felt the wig SHIFT forward onto my forehead. Now there's a pickle. And I got tickled because I didn't know what to do.

I couldn't see it. Had it slipped down enough that it was touching my eyebrows? Had anyone noticed? If they did, would they even say anything? Do I go ahead and grab it and put it back to its rightful position? What was it going to look like when I got up if I didn't go ahead and adjust it then? What if by then it was half way slipped off my head and my side part was now right above my ear? What IS proper etiquette for wig malfunction? For the time being, this is my life.

A couple of weeks ago, I went on a rare outing and took my son to Dexter. Knowing that at the time he was more comfortable with me when I have on my hair and because I love my kids, I put on my hair piece once more. Then I realized it was super windy outside and I was out of gas. So I had to call my mom.

"Mom, can I borrow your car?" I asked.

"Well, of course," she said. "Is there something wrong with yours?"

"Yeah, it's out of gas and I'm afraid if I go to put some in it, the wind is going to blow my wig off."

Nuff said. I've made the executive decision to stick with my head scarves for now.

Being bald and free in the privacy of my own home has its drawbacks too though. One day, home alone, I was in the living room where there is a lovely bay window and forgot myself and left my head scarf in the bedroom. I was talking to my friend Nicole on the phone and suddenly there was a knock at the door! AND I WAS BALD! I jumped up and took off running and ended up in the kitchen.

"Oh no!" I told Nicole. "I've got my bald head shinin' and someone's at the door and I panicked and ran the wrong way! My scarves are in the bedroom and I'm in the stupid kitchen!"

She laughed and said "It's probably my sister. She said she was coming out."

So I grabbed a dish towel out of the drawer and covered my head and streaked through the house to the bedroom, scrambling for a scarf. By the time I got to the door,

Heather was getting in her car and I waved her back in.

"I'm sorry," I said, out of breath. "I was sitting here bald as I wanna be and when you knocked, I ran the wrong way and was trapped in the kitchen."

"I figured," she said, laughing. "I heard your feet pitter pattering through the house!"

The thing is I have come to realize that when my head is uncovered, I feel no different than I think I would at a topless beach. When my bald head is shining, as brazen as this sounds, I feel like I have a private part hanging out. It's ridiculous, but it's just the truth.

And anyway, if I did just decide to go Kojak, when I put my makeup on, am I supposed to put my foundation all over my head now so it matches my face? That could get expensive. Just a thought.

Back to the topic at hand though. It was during week 3 of chemo, when things were tough on me in so many ways, that I was overwhelmed with the feeling of embarrassment of not having hair, of the fact that because of the steroids they are giving me, I am as heavy now as I was when I was nearly full term with each of my kids. My clothes do not fit, and I don't feel cute in what few pieces I have that I CAN fit into. Unable to work, I am, in essence, not a nail technician right now. And having the heart of a nail tech, it's just adding insult to injury that my fingernails and toenails are not only neglected but may, during this whole mess, turn black or yellow and might even FALL OFF.

I don't want to be embarrassed of who I am or what I look like. I understand this isn't forever and that my hair will grow back, and I will lose this weight and whatever happens to my fingernails and toenails, if anything happens at all, will hopefully be temporary as well. I know it in my head. The rest of me just won't let it go.

I've decided though to try to gear my thought process to "What a great time for a fresh start!" Stripped bare I'm beginning to see myself for who I really am. Was I really a blonde ? (Of course not. I have great hair dressers.) But what I'm saying is, I've never had dark hair before. Maybe I'm bolder and more confident with dark hair. Maybe I'm "all that and a bag of chips" with dark hair.

With that physical slate wiped clean, I feel almost like I could just dump all the extra baggage of wishing I were stronger physically and emotionally, wishing I was more confident, wishing I loved more, laughed more, cried more, took more chances.

People want a fresh start, they move to a new state. I want a fresh start, I don't even have to pack a bag. I can just look in the mirror. I'll be a blank canvas and a palette full of paints. An empty journal and a brand new pen.

So here I am. Stripped of my unintentional disguise. Fat, skinny, bald or in a crooked wig, dressed to the nines or in my sweats, it's still me under all that.

And because this is part of the journey.......this is me. Stripped on the outside, a work in progress on the inside. But my heart beats the same.

Chapter 12

Every day's a holiday..., Every meal's a banquet...

Since I last wrote, I have completed three...count them...THREE more chemo treatments. And I realized on the way home from my last one how strange it has become. Strange because where the IDEA of chemo had become "just chemo," now the actual treatment itself (knock on wood) has begun to run like a well-oiled machine. With Kelley's encouragement, I have finally started to listen to the nurse's advice about really gooping on the numbing cream onto my port. Now even though I feel I am putting on a ridiculous amount, the needle placement feels like nothing. No pain at all. During my last lab work, my blood flowed like a champ. Also, I have had no adverse reactions to my new chemo. And seeing that the possibilities included becoming flushed, difficulty breathing, chest pain, back pain, pain in general, etc., I was pretty happy that for me, there has so far been nothing. The three or four pre-meds that I receive before the hour-long Taxol pack no wallop. And maybe it was because during this last chemo I was in a hospital bed under a blanket straight out of the warmer and not in a recliner this time, and maybe it was because of the rain falling outside the big window beside me, but whatever it was, the Benadryl came to me gently this time and closed my eyes offering a peaceful sleep. Other days it comes at me like a sledge hammer, making my eyes cross and my lips numb and making whatever conversation I am in the midst of when it hits very weird for everyone involved.

And the part where the doctor said these last 12 treatments would be easier than the first 4 aggressive ones has turned out to be fairly true. I look back now and can really see how heavy those first four were. I was living it, I suppose, and not really paying attention. Heck, I guess you could say I slept through them. It was just a few weeks ago that I would get up in the morning and simply the act of putting my makeup on exhausted me for the rest of the day. My eyes would close involuntarily at times and other times Kelley could see me crashing before I knew it was happening and he would direct me to the couch or to bed. I would huff off like a four year old, mad because he was telling me what to do, but he was always right and in about fifteen minutes I was out. Now I can make it through most days without even a nap. There's been a horizontal rest that has taken place a few times but it's not necessary for me to sleep for 20 minutes just to be able to continue a conversation with someone and although it was super sweet and made for fond memories, my friends don't have to camp out in bed with me now to visit because I'm too exhausted to sit up in the living room. I don't have to have the shots anymore that made me achy. But this chemo does just plain old make me hurt...all over. My stomach doesn't like it much either, but obviously it hasn't kept me from eating. All in all though, I'm doing fine.

Even the ice during Chemo #7 didn't seem unbearable. Oh...yes. The ice. I haven't mentioned the ice yet due to my lack of writing. My last musings talked of my sadness about the possibility of the new treatment, Taxol, robbing me of my nails. Knowing this might be an issue for me since nails are my business, my doctor was ready with a suggestion. Evidently, ice can restrict the blood flow to your nail beds which detours the chemo running through the veins past the nails, therefore reducing the possibility of damage. So, for my last three treatments, I have sat as long as I can stand through my hour-long Taxol, with my hands and feet in specimen bags full of ice. The first time eventually became a bit painful. The second time, instead of me putting my hands directly in the bags, we found a little pocket on the side so I wasn't directly in contact with the ice. Still yet though, the zippered closures sprung leaks and I ended up with cold and wet socks. During this last one though, Chemo #7, I made it for about 45 minutes before I had to thaw out. I wish there'd been an ice bath idea for my head. Maybe I wouldn't be bald right now. Anyhoo..........

Back to my deep thoughts of strange chemo...even though the Taxol is actually racing through my veins with the sole purpose of killing all the fast growing cells in my body, cancer cells or not, this latest treatment was painless and peaceful.

Now as I type this, Thanksgiving is over, decorations put away, leftovers trashed. Where has the time gone? In many ways, life has come to a complete standstill since my diagnosis. And then when I realize summer is long gone and now even Thanksgiving is behind us, I see time breezing by like the fanning pages of a book.

If I were being completely honest, I would have to say that when I was little, Thanksgiving was far from my favorite holiday. It was really only significant to me because we got out of school for it and because I knew it was a precursor to Christmas. There were no Thanksgiving baskets filled with candy left for me by the Thanksgiving Turkey, no Thanksgiving tree under which I could expect presents. It's a holiday decorated with CORN and other things brown and orange. And they generally didn't even sparkle. I didn't like pecan pie or vegetables or other Thanksgiving foods. Ornery little brat. What was wrong with me? Needless to say, as a grown-up, my outlook has changed. I love decorating for Thanksgiving. The orange of the pumpkins alongside the brilliant scarlet leaves of a red maple and yes, that gorgeous gold of a dried ear of corn. And maybe it was just that the food was extra super delicious at my Aunt Tamera's house and at my mother's this year, and maybe it was the steroids they're giving me, but either way, I ate A LOT, enjoyed every bite and was extremely thankful for another day spent with my sweet family.

And that's what Thanksgiving is all about - being thankful. I am glad that there is a day set aside in the year to remind us to be grateful, to take a minute and ponder the things we've taken for granted and forgotten to give a little thanks for. And my list is so long, especially this year, that I could NEVER complete it. I am thankful for big and obvious things, and I am grateful for tiny, minute and forgettable things.

For example, I am thankful that on Tuesday, when we went through a drive-thru for lunch, Kelley ordered a quarter pounder and when he opened it, they had given him a DOUBLE quarter pounder by mistake and hadn't charged us extra for it! See, even the small blessings are still blessings.

I am thankful that my son got to go with me to treatment last week so he can understand more of the experience and what it really means. And it was also just nice to have my handsome young man by my side.

I am thankful that I now have completed seven treatments total and that I only have nine left!!!!! I'm in the single digits now!!!

I am thankful beyond words, speechless and constantly moved to tears, by the outpouring of love and generosity we have received from our friends, from our church members, from the community, from people we had never met and now call "friend." I will always remember the text messages, the meals delivered to our home, the cards that each time I open them I read like a hug, the gifts and donations, the thoughts and prayers, the fundraisers our friends have thrown selling t-shirts, bracelets and chili and throwing the annual Halloween party all in the name of Operation Healthy Hooters, a TV raffled off at Kelley's work, and a delicious benefit dinner of ham and country fried steak that Bernie Express had for me, even serving me my own plate at a reserved table, decorated in pink, centered by a gorgeous flower arrangement just for me. I will never forget it. I don't think I'll ever be able to remember it without my emotions getting the best of me. I'll never stop shaking my head in wonder at the kindness and love we have been shown. And it seems impossible that I could ever repay all these kindnesses. All I can do is look forward to the day when I can begin paying it forward but until then, I'll just keep talking to God from bended knee, asking Him to pour his blessings out on all these special people in my life.

I am grateful for God's plan whether I understand it or not. I am grateful that my breast cancer was found early. I am grateful for the experience, that it has made me wiser, braver, stronger. And I am grateful for the lessons I have learned so far. I am grateful for the opportunity I have been blessed with to meet new people along this journey. Unforgettable people like Ms. Patsy, a fellow cancer patient who I have shared a pod with twice now. She doesn't know my name, but I've watched her enough to catch hers. She's one of those people whose presence in the room is so prominent. This strong woman who, as she receives her chemo, speaks with compassion and respect about the men she cooks for at the homeless shelter. I hear the pride in her voice when she talks about how they ask for her by name. This woman who fields calls from her family while she sits hooked up to an IV of cancer-killing poison, explaining to them what time she'll be home after her 4-5 hour chemo to cook them their favorite meal that they're craving. It's an act that she obviously adores; the requests taken not as a burden but as a joy that her food is the only food that seems to satisfy their hunger. And while her food feeds their souls, meeting a woman of her grace and caliber has fed mine.

I am thankful for the woman we met two weeks ago in pod 5, who talked all the while with a smile and upbeat demeanor of her Stage 4 cancer, of how she has moved from Illinois to receive her treatments and of how her daughter receives treatments for her own cancer still in Illinois because her four boys need her close. A mother and daughter fighting the same battle, yet in different rings. And yet she smiled as she spoke. How can I not gather strength from that? How could I not be grateful for that conversation, for that moment?

Thanksgiving is definitely the perfect time of year to be THANKFUL...yes!!! But as Kelley has said for years, "Every day's a holiday. Every meal's a banquet!"

Thanksgiving itself is gone for the year and today might just be another day, but I can guarantee somewhere in the midst of it, there's a blessing in there worth hanging on to.

Every day's a holiday. Every day that I live and breathe is beyond deeming as a blessing. Every moment that I hear "I love you" from my kids or my husband, that's a blessing not to be taken for granted. Every day I can find a reason to celebrate. I shouldn't just wait for a holiday to see it.

Every meal's a banquet. Whether it is a turkey dinner or an accidental double quarter pounder with cheese, a meal prepared by Ms. Patsy in a homeless shelter for men she doesn't know or the favorite foods she fixes in her own kitchen for her endless list of family and friends.

EVERY day is a holiday! EVERY meal is a banquet!

"Gratitude unlocks the fullness of life. It turns what we have into enough, and more. It turns denial into acceptance, chaos to order, confusion to clarity. It can turn a meal into a feast, a house into a home, a stranger into a friend. Gratitude makes sense of our past, brings peace for today, and creates a vision for tomorrow." -- Melody Beattie

Chemo #5, #6, and #7 - history.

Chemo #5

Chemo #6

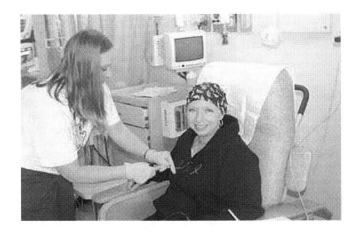

And Chemo #7

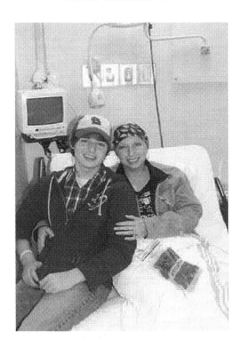

Chapter 13

Oh....my....word...

Fear.

If I looked hard, waded through the muck, fought through the jungle of emotion, wildly chopping all the foliage that entangled me to get to the real heart of what I felt in the beginning, there at the clearing lay fear.

I was afraid of what I didn't know, of what would lie ahead. Cancer and chemotherapy were such frightening words. The movie *Beaches* or *Terms of Endearment* broke my heart and set me on crying jags for hours. And all I could remember of those tear jerking favorites of mine were that the ones with cancer died. I didn't remember any scenes about chemotherapy or radiation. My only frames of reference of females with cancer were movies where the heroine lost. And now I was playing the lead role in my own movie.

Yes. I was now fighting cancer. I got that. Now just tell me HOW! They told me I would have surgery to remove it and I bailed off into that one. Now it's gone and I didn't understand how to fight what is next.

Would I be quarantined as I got chemotherapy? Would I have to be put under to receive it? Would I begin to throw up as soon as the chemo enters my veins? Would I wither away to nothing, a skeleton my children didn't recognize? Would I lose all strength and would Kelley have to carry me everywhere I went, from bed to couch to car? Would I be able to get out of bed at all?

The unknown is such a frightening place - so dark and consuming, dirty hands pulling you deeper and deeper into the quicksand of fear.

I suppose it was the fear in my voice that the nurse at my oncologist's office heard one day when I called that made her share a video with me.

"What's your email address?" she asked. "I'm going to send you a video that one of our patients made while she was getting treatment here."

When the email came, I didn't want to watch it. She had breast cancer just like me. I didn't know how much I could take. I didn't know what seeing the reality of it all would do to me. My mind had no choice but to run on the possibilities, but what if seeing this woman sick in bed, gray in pallor, void of hair, what if it was too much and the strength I had evaporated and I caved to the unknown? I thought the unknown was bad. But maybe the knowing would be worse.

The email haunted me. It hung over my head until I finally sat in front of the computer and hit play.

And cried all the way through.

It was about five minutes long maybe and better than any blockbuster I had ever seen. It was a video of strength and courage and, what I least expected, JOY! It was simply a slideshow set to music, showing the fight of a woman with breast cancer. A timeline of her battle, photos of each of her chemo treatments, a smile on her face, her fingers held to number the treatment. Photos of her cutting her hair short, of Christmas with her family, her last chemo, her tying her shoe as she prepared to, of all things, run a race, hair that she had lost now in full bloom on her head. The verse "Don't be afraid, just believe." – Mark 5:36 scattered throughout the video.

This woman I would never know had led the way, blazoned a path for me, sparked my hope and my fight, and she didn't even know it.

I was renewed and ready. The unknown was no longer my villain. The battlegrounds were clear now. This stranger had helped point out to me the task at hand and because of her I was ready.

As I wrote my blog, I found strength in myself as I put into words the journey I was on. And following in the footsteps of my new hero, I had Kelley take my picture at each chemotherapy to mark my own timeline and posted them with the story of each treatment.

The comments people left on my blog bolstered me. In the beginning, the words I wrote were so I would never forget the details of my own story. I never imagined the strength I would receive from the words of friends and strangers that took the time to comment.

Some said I was an inspiration. Others wrote encouraging words saying keep it up or that they were thinking about me. Some were strangers saying they enjoyed reading my story.

And there is one particular comment that I will never forget.

A woman from Van Buren, about an hour and a half from my home, had received the link to my blog from her sister who had seen it on her child's pediatrician's Facebook page. The pediatrician happened to be one of my best friends, Cory. Her sister had wanted her to read it because it had reminded her so much of the blog she had started in August of 2008, a blog she had started a month before receiving her own breast cancer diagnosis. No family history, just like me. She had completed her treatments and assured me she was doing well, giving me her email address and the link to her own blog. *Stay strong, girl! You've SO got this!* she wrote.

Another survivor with a blog. Another fighter's story. I was a member of a new club, and it was an honor for me to read about her fight.

I pulled up her blog, smiled at the picture of her and her family and began to read. But my eyes were drawn again and again to this photo. This smiling woman with her happy family.

And then it hit me.

It couldn't be.

But it was.

The woman who had commented on my blog was the very woman whose video had bolstered my spirit, readied me for battle, a stranger I was never to meet who had no idea that I had ever been sent the email that changed me.

So unbelievable, I needed some time to grasp it, to absorb the wonder of it.

God knew I had been afraid. He saw me frightened. And so He sent me a gift, the gift of hope and peace I received from watching this woman's journey, showing me I was going to be all right. And then to give me proof, He had been there all along; He led Erica and I to one another.

Finally the words that I wanted to pass on to my new friend came to me and I began to write.

Erica,

I am constantly amazed at how God works. Sometimes it just makes me shake my head and giggle.

In the beginning of this scary journey, before I started chemo, a nurse at Siteman took a moment out of her day to email a link to a slideshow of an amazing woman and her own journey through cancer. I was so frightened and had no idea what to expect of chemo and cancer and as I watched this slideshow I cried and I cried. But this woman in these pictures had paved the way for me, painting a picture of what things would be like, giving me strength and courage and made me feel like I wasn't alone in this.

Every time you see a photo of me in my blog where I hold up my fingers to show my countdown, it is even then that I carried the strength of this fellow fighter with me.

I saw your picture and felt as if I knew you already. And then I realized that it was you that had been by my side in spirit this whole time and I thought to myself "There you are!" as if I'd been waiting for our paths to cross this whole time.

I am so glad that I've been given the opportunity to thank you. Maybe your slideshow was just for your own benefit, to ensure that you never forget all that you went through, but being able to watch it was a gift to me because it took away some of my fears and let me take a deep breath.

So, thank you Erica, from the bottom of my heart! I am so proud of your courage and your fight. You are an amazing woman and I am forever grateful to you!

Love, Becky

And her response:

Becky,

Just about all I can say is "Oh...my...word...". When I got your email today I was sitting in the high school parking lot waiting to pick up my oldest son from basketball practice and my jaw was standing wide open while I was reading it! I am over the top stunned. I don't know what to say except to completely echo your words of "shake my head and giggle". Isn't our god so amazing?! I've often said that my most favorite thing to do is to stand back and watch Him work. It is simply amazing. I am in awe. I could just cry! God is so cool. Truly.

Yeah. He sure is.

And it would also be cool to be able to write here that from bended knee I asked God for a sign that He was watching over me, that I was afraid and I needed His help and He sent me Erica. But you know what's even cooler? I didn't. I didn't have to. You see, He knew what I needed before I did. He already had it all in place, just waiting for the right time to reveal the good works, the GOD works that He had ready for me.

I was afraid of the unknown, of the dark ahead of me. And He turned on the light.

"I will lead the blind by a way that they do not know. I will lead them in paths they do not know. I will turn darkness into light in front of them. And I will make the bad places smooth. These are the things I will do and I will not leave them."

--Isaiah

42:16

Chapter 14

Wait a minute…

The day after Thanksgiving, my heart was all aflutter. It skipped a beat and went pitter pat. No, really. My heart started skipping beats. Or, as it turns out, was throwing in an extra one. Boom, boom, boom…boom, boom, boom. I describe it and it makes me picture Patrick Swayze holding my hand to his chest, "Gagung…gagung." With every break in my rhythm, my chest felt tight or heavy and sometimes I would get pretty lightheaded.

I am a self-diagnoser. There has to be a 12 step program for that. I hate going to the doctor and leaving knowing there really wasn't anything seriously wrong with me in the first place, realizing if I'd waited another day or so and just toughed it out, it would have gone away on its own. So when it started, Dr. Beck attributed all strange heart flutterings to extreme intake of caffeine. The very first time it happened I had just taken a big gulp of Diet Pepsi and remember even telling Kelley later that my first morning's jolt of caffeine had messed me up somehow.

The week wore on and it seemed to be a little better. I ignored it when it cut my Christmas shopping outing to Wal-Mart short, frustrated because it wasn't often that I got out and about and I had to return home early. By then the end of the week, I decided it wasn't caffeine after all. It was surely anxiety. I mean, come on. I've been through a lot in the last few months, and I haven't run away screaming yet. It would only make sense for me to be a little emotional or anxious or out of control to where it might affect me physically.

The second Sunday after Thanksgiving, I got up and

got our stuff ready for a family photo session with Julie Dodd. Ironed shirts, accessorized, brushed hair (I know, not my own), and by the time we were halfway there, my heart beat was all over the place and I was worn out. Anxiety. Of course. I'm in a tizzy. I've got to calm down. We arrived at Julie's, had a great time, got back in the car and it started again. It was surely all in my mind.

We drove on and dropped Mallory at her Christmas program practice, grabbed lunch, came home and I didn't really want to talk about it but something just wasn't right. I secretly checked my blood pressure because I didn't want Kelley to panic. It was fine except when my heart fluttered, the blood pressure machine I had borrowed from my mother couldn't do a reading and would just stop and say *EE*. I never knew what that meant and when Google produced nothing, I did the only thing I could think of and I changed the battery.

Exhausted, I ended up taking a two-hour nap after Kelley and I fussed for a bit. I could pretend we didn't argue about it, just leave that part out. But if I'm not going to be real about how it really happened, then why tell the story at all. We argued because we were scared. I was too scared to admit something wasn't right and he was scared because I wouldn't go get checked out, and the head butt began. A battle of wills. Who won? I really couldn't say. We both had our shining moments. And since in the end, I DID go get checked out, I suppose I shall concede and give the victory to Kelley. But he'll have to read this book to find out about that because I'm sure not going to tell him.

Back to my flutters. After my nap, I jumped up, spruced myself up a bit and everyone else too and we headed to Mal's Christmas program. It was wonderful. Afterward, we went to enjoy a great meal at the Mexican restaurant, and while I was there, my heart fluttered so strongly that I wasn't positive that my head hadn't physically swayed when I felt like I was blacking out a bit. By the time we got home and got the kids to bed and Kelley and I had some quiet time to discuss what was happening, I gave in and told him to call my mom. I packed a "just in case" bag and at around 11:00 pm, we headed out to the hospital ER.

Not long after arriving at the emergency room, we were taken back and (surprise) I was handed a gown to put on. Then after describing my symptoms, an EKG, chest x-ray and CT scan were ordered. I simply saw dollar signs. Nothing is ever wrong with me. Wait…isn't this kind of how I started this whole cancer story in the first place? Anyway, the EKG was quick, and it wasn't long before two men came in wheeling with them the machine for the chest x-ray. Now remember, I am a nail technician, so I won't act like I know what I'm talking about because I don't. I'll simply describe what they did in Becky terms. They sat me up and placed some kind of board behind my back and as they left the room to take the actual x-ray, I realized I looked straight ahead at the machine and SMILED. I smiled for the chest x-ray. And when the first one wasn't to their satisfaction and they repeated the process, I'll be dadgum if I didn't do it again! It was involuntary! A lifetime of smiling for the camera left me to pose and smile for a photo that was obviously NOT going to show my face. Thank goodness Kelley wasn't in there and the men didn't notice, or at least they didn't mention it even as they wheeled me down for the CT scan.

After the tests were complete and I was back in the room I shared with a little elderly woman and her granddaughters, the two of us only divided by a curtain, I was in need of the lady's room. See, here's the thing about me. My bladder is the size of a grape. I'm the girl who has visited every public restroom in a two hundred mile radius of her home. So here I am, at the ER, having endured a 30-minute drive, a 10-15 minute wait in the waiting room, and then the time that had passed while we sat in the room and I had had tests run and smiled cheerily for a chest x-ray. I had to GO!

However, seeing that there was no bathroom in the room we were in and also seeing that I was still hooked to all kinds of monitors, I had Kelley go ahead and alert the nurse that I needed to use the restroom.

"The doctor doesn't want you to get out of bed," the nurse said, "but I can bring you a potty chair."

Curious as to why I couldn't get out of bed, I accepted it as hospital procedure. Kelley and I, always easy-going, never ones to question anything right away, both simply thanked her and smiled until she was out of the room. My face immediately fell as I looked at Kelley and said "Are you kidding me?" He smirked and turned his head, I'm sure already aware that in my mind this was all his fault for pressing me to come to the ER and that he would pay for this. Either he was going to be buying me something pretty or I was at least reserving the right to bring this up at any time in the future that it seemed to suit me.

As the nurse brought in the chair, she placed it in the only space available, up against the curtain. Do I need to remind you about the fact that on the other side of the curtain were PEOPLE? I sent Kelley to the doorway to head anyone off that might attempt to interrupt my potty respite. I wrestled with my gown and the many wires running in and out of the sleeves and neck. I tried to put aside from my mind the audience that I knew was listening and wished I knew meditation or some other technique to coax my shy bladder into action. By the time my body decided to cooperate, the sound was like a water hose hitting the empty bottom of a 55 gallon drum and I got tickled, causing the sound to resemble the deep hum of a hillbilly band playing the jug. By the time Kelley stepped back through the curtain, the stress of the whole experience so far and the middle of the night slap-happies ascended upon us and we laughed until we cried, especially when he revealed he could even hear me in the hall.

Soon, the ER doctor joined us and said it was good that we had come in. The CT scan showed I had multiple small blood clots in my lower left lung and tiny ones around those. I remember the doctor saying how she just hated to have to give me news like that because I was so sweet. I couldn't figure out where she'd come up with that. I didn't remember being sweet. I remember expecting Kel and I to get kicked out at any moment because we were laughing way too loud. Our conversations with the doctor had been brief. We asked questions. She answered them. Actually, we thought SHE was the sweet one.

It wasn't long before they wheeled me down the hall to ICU. I really enjoyed the nurses in the ER. Now I was off to meet a new crew, make some new friends.

Anyone who knows me knows that Matthew McConaughey is my boyfriend. Ok, well, we're seeing each other. Ok, well, not really. I mean, I see him. On TV and in the occasional magazine. He has no idea and would most likely be disturbed or find cause to have me arrested or at least put a restraining order on me of some kind. Anyway, after they settle me into my ICU bed and Kelley joined me, he said, "Hey Beck, this guy out here has something to show you." The guy he was referring to worked in the ICU and was sporting a *Just Keep Livin'* bracelet. I recognized the motto immediately as a signature line from Matthew McConaughey and that I recognized from his website. Not because I'm a stalker or anything. I can't help it that I'm on his mailing list and that he sends me emails! Later the guy came to my bedside with the bracelet in his hand and offered it to me.

"Would you wear it?" he asked.

"Of course!" I said. I wondered later if he and I might be married now. In some country somewhere, my acceptance of that bracelet surely means I accidentally joined him in holy matrimony. But it didn't really matter because in that little bed in the early morning hour, I lay there all a glow with Matthew McConaughey's vibes on my wrist. Just keep livin'. Ok. I can do that. All right all right all right.

What was I talking about again? Oh yes! Blood clots. In my lungs.

The people that took care of me in ICU were AWESOME. They went above and beyond even down to the sweet nurse who left me her 2 liter of Diet Pepsi when her shift was over or Steve, the nurse who was with me for the day who called me "Little Lady." But as precious as they were, my oncologist preferred I was in St. Louis where he could monitor me closely so he put in an order for my transfer. In order to get there though, I had to take a ride in an ambulance. My first and only ambulance ride. Of course all I could think about was the bags of fluids they'd been giving me, the fact that the ride was going to be a good 2 ½ hours and there is NO bathroom on an ambulance. So my first question to the two ambulance drivers was, "So are we stopping at Burger King when I need a potty break?"

"That's where WE stop," they replied, comfortingly.

And as I climbed onto the gurney, one of them said, "Jamie told us we were supposed to take extra special care of you." A friend of a friend that I had yet to meet had been sweet enough to send some "handle with care" instructions.

As strange as it sounds, the parts I remember of my ambulance ride (due to the medication they'd given me in preparation for my travels), I fairly enjoyed. The lights inside looked slightly like disco lights and the bumpy ride rocked me to sleep. The guys that accompanied me took great care of me. We joked and I laughed a lot. Especially when it was about 20 below and I was in nothing but a gown on a gurney, and they got me out and tried to deliver me to the wrong building. They loaded me up again and off we went once again this time to the right place. I felt silly laying on that gurney while they pushed me around. I wasn't sick and it felt unnecessary and I just wanted to say, "Here, I really can walk all by myself!" But they couldn't let me do that. So I behaved and cooperated and giggled uncontrollably when they decided to try and fit us, two guys and a girl on a gurney, through the revolving doors to get into the hospital, the steady spin coming to a halt every few feet, a voice repeatedly saying, "Please step forward." Good times.

They were super sweet and I was sad to see them go, but they had to get back home and it was time to get back to the business at hand.

To sum it up, after many tests, echocardiograms, ultrasounds of my arms and legs, a 24-hour heart monitor, I was released a couple of days later. There was no sign of any more clots in my legs or arms that would be of significant danger and over time blood thinners would help prevent more clots, and my body would in time absorb the clots in my lungs. I left on a regimen of Lovenox shots in which Kelley gives me in my lower abdomen twice a day. They burn and they bruise me. I look like a leopard. I don't like them at all, and Kelley seems to hate giving them to me worse. But the plan is that I'll do them for 6-8 months.

It was so good to be home. The doctors said that it was fine to move and exercise. There was no more need for bed rest which was wonderful! But by Friday my heart was still fluttering, and I was becoming short of breath so back to the ER we went. Earlier in the week, I met that challenge with a smile. But on Friday, I had lost my resolve and when Kelley gave me my shot that morning, I cried. And tears haven't been a part of this for some time now. And when in the ER, I told them to go ahead and access my port even though I knew there hadn't been time for the numbing cream to take effect yet, the pain was overwhelming and I cried once more, feeling so terrible for the nurse who watched the tears that she was unwillingly causing. And later that night, after they had sent me home saying my CT scan from that day was normal and Kelley gave me my second shot of the day, even though I tried to hide it from him by pulling my toboggan over my eyes, he caught me crying then too.

Such an enormously stressful week on top of what I was already going through. The weight of the whole journey bearing down heavy on me already and then thrown over the edge by the fear and anxiety I had just endured during the week, the disappointment of being told I couldn't do my chemo that week, feeling desperate for it like an addict of some kind. A chemo junky? No. But not getting my chemo that week meant the end date of my treatments I'd been so focused on was now extended by a week. It was almost too much. Almost.

Sometimes I need a minute. A break. A vacation from cancer, from chemo, from blood clots, from shots, from thinking thoughts, from running in circles all day, from going really big and seeming to get nowhere fast. I just want to step out of it all for a minute. Just let me catch my breath. Can you just let me catch my breath for a minute? But there is no break and no breather. Not in this fight.

But I found the words I needed, the encouragement to sort it all out and start fresh without being able to break from the battle.

"But those who trust in the Lord will renew their strength; they will soar on wings like eagles; they will run and not grow weary; they will walk and not faint."

--Isaiah 40:31

It is God's grace that has carried me this far, given me the strength to get to this point. I look back at how far I have come and think no wonder I'm tired and wish to stop, to just wait a minute and start fresh. But the promise has been made to me that I shall walk and not faint. So I'll continue on down the path I'm traveling, at peace knowing no matter how fast I feel like I'm running, or how out of breath I might feel, my strength will be renewed. The battle is not done. And neither am I.

"If in your sickness you are desperate to recover
Wait a minute, wait a minute, wait a minute now
When you're a seeker who is longing to discover
Wait a minute, wait a minute, wait a minute now,
Cause
They who wait on the Lord shall renew their strength
They will mount up on wings

They will walk and not faint
Seasons of this life change but God's faithfulness remains
They who wait on the Lord shall renew their strength."
--Wait A Minute by Big Daddy Weave

Chapter 15

I was here...

The other day I passed Ryan in the hallway and he stopped me, putting his hands on my arms and turning me to face him. He studied my face for a moment and then said, "Ya know, I can't really see your eyebrows anymore!"

I knew it was coming. I had gone and bought an eyebrow pencil the week before because a small bald spot had appeared in one brow and I knew what was next.

The next morning my alarm woke me to start my day and as I got up, there in the bathroom mirror, my sleepy eyes were greeted by someone who looked like a cancer patient.

Good morning, Beck.

The cancer look has come in installments, each dose just enough for me to handle, not enough to send me over the edge, although the latter was questionable on occasion. At this point in the game though, I have come to terms I think with the changes my body has gone through and is STILL going through. And having just completed my 8th treatment of 16, I feel I've cleared the top of my chemo mountain, and though the road the rest of the way is bound to have its twists and turns, the rest is still downhill from here.

I could wish this away. I could click my heels three times and hope to open my eyes on July 15, 2011, a year from the day of my diagnosis, when most likely the monumental parts of the journey are over, when I no longer feel like every time I sit down next to my IV pole, an imaginary announcer points to me and says, "And in THIS CORNER..."

But if I fast forward, what a wasted trip! Do I want to do this again? HECK NO! And yes, there are parts of this that hurt to think about and are painful to remember, and yes there are parts I'm still dreading, but I don't want to forget it.

My hair is growing back right now and oddly everything is coming back in the order it fell out. And even that might be temporary since I have 8 more treatments to go. But Friday, on our way home from St. Louis, I had on a toboggan and when I pulled it off in the car to let my head breathe, I rubbed my hand over my head and then snatched down the visor to look in the mirror. I sat up straight in my seat and exclaimed, "Kel, my hair is a MESS!!" I was so proud!

My eyebrows and eyelashes are disappearing. I have had conversations in the last few days with people in which I have had to stop and say, "Excuse me, my eyelashes are falling out as we speak," and I would fish one out of my eyeball as I continued our conversation.

My new friend, Julie, a very gifted photographer, offered to take pictures for me, to document this time in my life. We had graduated the same year but attended different schools in different towns. Because she, a volleyball player in high school and me ....um....NOT one, due to issues with ....um....my ability to never hit a ball coming even directly at me, we probably don't necessarily have memories of one another from back then. But truth be told, we most likely were at a lot of the same games and functions and just never knew it. Then over 15 years later, after reading my blog and talking to some friends we had in common, she reached out to me via email, introduced herself and made an offer to do a photo session if I ever felt up to it. We bonded immediately and even now we joke about how we are such kindred spirits and that it's hard to remember not knowing one another.

It was only a week or so before receiving her email that I had gone outside and set up a backdrop in our fenced-in backyard. I set my self-timer on my camera, attempting on my own to capture the images I had in my head of my bald self in a tank top and pink boxing gloves. I'd push the button on the camera, run like the wind to my spot, wait for the click of the shutter, review the image and then click and run again. In the end, I had come away with nothing more than a bunch of photos of me looking like I wanted to hurt someone and I kinda did. The wind was blowing and the backdrop fell on my head more than once. I was never able to get the shot I wanted. I wanted fierce...resolute...and instead I got frustrated and sweaty.

So the timing of her email and her offer was perfect and I took her up on it. I explained to her about my idea for photos of me with my bald head shining, wearing pink boxing gloves, and she was more than willing to help me fulfill my vision. So two Sundays in a row, she took a few hours out of her day to help me freeze some moments during this journey. What a blessing and a gift.

I have always loved photos. Time travels so fast. Things change in the blink of an eye, and you just want to stop time and say *Wait a minute*. Kids grow up and their looks change, special moments we hope to never forget play out, loved ones we can't imagine living without are here one second and gone the next. Photos secure that memory forever. Proof that yes, I really did wear my hair like that on purpose. Proof that we WERE young once. Proof that my kids were once chubby, slobbering babies. Proof that I once met a celebrity. Proof that holidays were special for my kids and that we loved summer vacation at the beach. Proof that I had cancer. Proof that I fought. Proof that I laughed and loved and lived. Proof that I existed, making my mark in time. Becky was here.

In the end, it turns out that when Julie took photos for us, she was able to snap shots of me and my family at such a poignant time in my life. It has been a difficult path we have traveled so far, but I am proud of this life. Every snap of her camera stopped time, saving a moment out of my journey as we might snatch a blown kiss from someone out of the air and tuck it in our pocket for safe keeping. And when the dust clears and I look back to see where I've been, I now have more than just words and memories to prove that …

   I was here.

   --"*I wanna try to touch a few hearts in this life*
   And leave nothing less than something that says 'I was
here'"

   I Was Here Lady Antebellum

Chapter 16

Let's cha cha...

It was only six months ago that I had long, blonde hair and a tan from the sun. I weighed around 125 lbs. and I had two complete eyebrows. Today I weigh...not 125 lbs., and I have one thinning eyebrow and another that is missing the last half and also a patch in that little dewdrop of a swoop where the eyebrow begins. You know, the best part. I am beyond pale. I don't even know what color to call this. And my hair is taunting me.

I look back now at how terrifying and traumatizing it was to not only lose my hair, but to know it was going to happen. My mother always told me that when she was a little girl and she went to get a shot, her country doctor would stomp on her foot when he stuck her with the needle. The pain of a stomped foot always distracted from the pain of the shot. That's quite a theory. Come to think of it, maybe God has been using that method on me. I was so distracted by the thought that my hair was going to come out and then the fact that it DID, the cancer part of this deal played second fiddle a lot. So I say to Him, "Well played."

How many times have I looked at a picture of myself and seen nothing but that one hair out of place and fussed because it just ruined the whole thing? How often did the hint of a double chin make me dismiss a photo and hope to never see it again because if anyone saw it, they would think I was really letting myself go? I had smiled too big. I hadn't smiled enough. That color just wasn't right on me, and I vowed never to wear it again. My nose looked big-ger than usual. Is that eye smaller than the other?

I was NEVER perfect. I was never a supermodel. But I was normal and average, and I miss being those things.

In the last six months, I've had to go buy bigger clothes so many times that I have finally just stopped. For Christmas, Kelley bought me some comfortable elastic wind pants and sweatshirts. They are actually in men's sizes because trying to find clothes to fit me comfortably in women's sizes just seems to be enhancing the trauma. I am still doing the Lovenox shots in my lower abdomen twice a day and I stay so bruised and sore that wearing jeans is just too painful. I am also blaming the shots on my lower belly being larger than usual. I do not have it on anyone's authority that this is a medical possibility. I have cancer and my pants don't fit. Please do not argue with me.

I weigh more than I have ever weighed now, even more than when I gave birth to my children. I got on the treadmill today and could feel my belly moving as I ran/walked. See, I can't even call it running. I don't think it could even be constituted as a jog. It was a ralk. And as bad as that sounds, I can GUARANTEE it looked even worse. Also, while I was visiting with a friend earlier today, our conversation led me to want to shake my head vehemently from side to side. At this point in the game, I SHOULD NEVER DO THAT! I felt the movement and as if time began to slow, I was picturing in my head what my chins were doing. And I say chins because I swear it's more than a double chin, and I've never heard of a triple and don't care to claim ownership of the first. It must have been swinging from side to side like that dog on *Turner and Hooch* that slung slobber with every shake of his head.

Also, this last chemo, for whatever reason, made my face break out terribly. It happened before in earlier chemos but sporadically and never twice in a row. Each treatment sends me home with a surprise symptom or symptoms. It's like chemo roulette or a quick game of spin the wheel for your discomfort. "Let's see what she's playing for this week, Ted!" So when December 30 arrived, I shouldn't have been surprised when chemo 11 made me much more tired than usual, and made me break out like I have just hit puberty.

And then there's my hair. I used to have a birthday card I kept forever with the sweetest baby orangutan on it. She wore a diaper and her hair just stuck up straight off of her head! I may not be wearing a diaper (and I am sooo grateful), but I look in the mirror and I see that orangutan.

I go to sleep every night with a toboggan under my pillow. And I can honestly say I never expected to say those words. However, it is a true statement. I have several toboggans now that I wear around the house and I change them up often. Whether it is hot flashes due to the chemotherapy or just the fact that toboggans aren't necessarily MADE to be worn inside OR worn to bed, I hop in the sack ready to get cozy and warm, and in a few seconds, am already throwing back the covers and tucking my toboggan of choice for the night under my pillow for safekeeping, so that in the wee hours of the morning when my bald little head begins to ache from the cold air, I am prepared and can quickly remedy the situation before things get out of hand and I'm awake for the rest of the night.

I have just enough hair right now that I almost just want to wipe it off. It's there and it catches the eye. But it's just sparing enough that from a distance my head still shines like a new penny. I stand in the mirror and examine the madness. I take two steps back and admire the shine. Two steps forward and I see the fact that there is more on one side than there is on the other. Two steps back and a squint, I see I look like a dandelion. Just makes me want to take a deep breath and blow! Two steps forward again and it's obvious my hair on the sides is dark and the hair on the top is white except for that bald spot in the back. Two steps back, I take a look at the whole picture and I see what others must see if I catch their eye. I see a round, bald woman, with no eyebrows and very countable eyelashes. Two steps forward. Two steps back. It's like a cha cha.

There's no stopping it. I read somewhere that chemotherapy will age you 10 years. It's happening fast enough already. I don't need any help! But there it is. What will I be like when it's all finished? When the bell has been rung and these chemicals are washed clean from my system, will my hair grow at lightning speed and my hind end deflate back to its pre-cancer shape? Once upon a time if I gained five pounds, I could skip a few meals and it would melt away on its own. Simply turning 35 had already changed that. An extra five pounds was going to stick around unless I concentrated a little. So I can only imagine what MULTIPLE sets of five pounds will be like to make disappear.

All of that though is for another day. This is who I am right now. I can't put a lot of thought or effort into what is to come. I have five more chemos to go and my focus has to be on finishing what I've started. When it's all said and done, I'll pick up the pieces and do some damage control.

Until then, the popular saying says to "dance like no one is watching." So I will.

"Optimist: someone who figures that taking a step backward after taking a step forward is not a disaster, it's a cha-cha."

--Robert Brault

Chemo is changing me on the outside. But because of chemo, I'm still here so that change is even a possibility.

Now let's cha-cha.

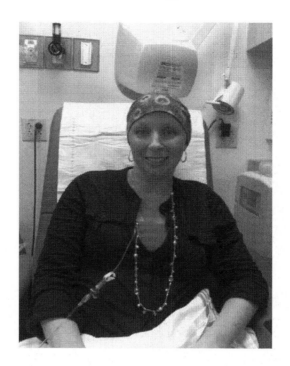

Chemo 11…danced.

Chapter 17

Running from the monster…

In three days I'll pull on my boxing gloves and bang them together like fighters do and I'll bound into the "ring" for the last time. This Friday is my very last chemo. Now that I can see the end of this leg of the journey, I suppose I am letting these walls I have built up over the last 6 months begin their retreat. Flashes of moments I have lived and yet filed away have fluttered across my mind's eye more and more since last week's trip to St. Louis.

I didn't realize the death grip I had on it all. I have joked about my denial about the whole thing and yet to a certain extent, even if it's not denial, I see I have had to mentally remove myself from the whole shebang.

You know the girl in the scary movies, always running from the monster…in high heel shoes….clop clop clop clop clop, making a bunch of racket,falling down a lot because she's running in high heel shoes. And she's forever stopping and turning around to see how close he is behind her, to see if she's been successful in giving him the slip. All the while she's SCREAMING, alerting this fool to her whereabouts with her hysterical squeals and noisy footsteps.

I hate that girl.

I could picture myself though, for the last few months, in my own scary movie. And in this movie it's ME being chased by the monster. But I threw my heels in the bushes. I've bitten permanent teeth marks in my lips stifling my screams. I feel as if I've been running…as if my life depended on it…too afraid to look back and see how far I had come…because if I stumbled…if I fell…I didn't know if I would get back up again.

Friday I will sit for the final time in that chair, receive my premeds and the Benadryl I have formed a love/hate relationship with, for the last time, and then I'll watch that bag of chemo disappear into my port.

I am trying to get a handle on my emotions, on my thoughts. Clear it out, let it loose, wash it clean. But I don't think I'm there yet. This part of the scary movie isn't done yet. The music is building. I think I've gone far enough and run hard enough that I have lost the monster. I outran him, zigged when he zagged. I can see the way out, like I'm racing down a dark hallway, the light under the door to safety as my only guide.

I can't look back yet though. I can't open my heart and my mind to the memories just yet and see how far I have come. Not yet. Because what if I crack, lose my resilience, my focus? I cannot falter.

But I was never alone even when fear clouded my vision. God never intended for me to feel as if I was running from the enemy. He had already given me every weapon I needed to defeat them.

"Above all, taking the shield of faith with which you will be able to quench all the fiery darts of the wicked one. And take the helmet of salvation, and the sword of the Spirit, which is the word of God"

--Ephesians 6:16, 17

When that last bag of chemo runs dry, when I am freed from the "chains" of the IV, when I walk out of that pod and ring that bell, I'll be slamming that door in cancer's face, clicking the lock, leaving the monster in the darkness for my eternity.

And may the ring of the bell, clanged by my hand, be a battle cry to the rest of my warrior friends and to the monsters they are locking up tight.

"Be sober, be vigilant; because your adversary the devil walks about like a roaring lion, seeking whom he may devour. Resist him,

steadfast in the faith, knowing that the same sufferings are experienced by your brotherhood in the world." -- 1 Peter: 8, 9

Chapter 18

And He came running...

Sixteen chemotherapy treatments total was the task set in front of me. But the shock and excitement on my face would have been the same if I had just won a Grammy when right before I went to begin Chemo #14, Dr. Pluard, my oncologist, told me that I didn't have to make up the treatment I missed when I was in the hospital due to the blood clots. "So after today you only have one more," he said. And I could have kissed him square on the mouth.

I have lost count on hotel stays for us so I have no number assigned to this particular night here at the Drury. I suppose what really counts, though, is tomorrow. Tomorrow is January 28. Tomorrow is chemo #15. Tomorrow is the last one. The bell ringer.

Tonight is a night for reflection, I suppose. As much as I have looked forward to tomorrow for the last five months, I have also thought of this night. Maybe tonight I will be able to let down my guard a bit, give myself permission to look over my shoulder and see how far I have come. Until now even the very idea was most days too painful. I needed to wait until the coast was clear before I unlocked the vault, before I gave the OK to start the memory montage that is bound to come flooding in. Even now as I write this, things are locked up fairly secure. I have kept a tight rein on things, waiting for this night, when I knew for sure that I had accomplished what I had set out to do. For my children, for my husband, for my parents, for my family and for my friends who love me so much, I set out to make this go away. Tomorrow when I ring that bell, they can rest assured that although the battle is not over, this round is finished. And I won.

I remember receiving the call that day. My memory montage begins for now after the conversation itself, fast forwarded to the moment I hung up the phone. Home alone, like standing on the state line, being in two places at once, it was as if I was straddling my reality. My body had cancer. My mind didn't know about it yet. I called Kelley, who was at my mom's, and tried to ask him calmly to come home. But those words set the ball rolling. The words sent up the flare that made it too late.

"Can you go ahead and come home?"

"Why? What's wrong?"

"Nothing, can you just come home?"

I wanted to stay in a state of oblivion, and I could have for a little while longer. But making the call changed the tides and I knew it. Somehow I sensed that I had only a precious few minutes left, where the news was mine. Where what I knew had knocked the wind out of me, it hadn't reached the ones I loved yet. I could only imagine Kelley's reaction. I could only imagine my parents' heartbreak. I had a few minutes before I said the words that were going to change everything.

So I went to the bathroom and I locked the door. I closed the lid on the toilet and sat down. And with head bowed and hands clasped I simply said, "God, this is too big for me. So I'm just going to give it to you."

I knew there were scriptures that would tell me He could do it. I knew there were scriptures that would tell me He WOULD. But I didn't know what they were or where to find them. I just knew it was more than I could handle on my own, more than I HAD to handle on my own. I am not perfect. Even my FAITH is far from perfect. But God heard my cry. And He smiled and came running.

We watch our children roll over, crawl, fight to walk. Their tiny hands hold ours as they build strength and confidence in their wobbly legs and when they take a spill, we help them up and offer our hands again until they find their balance.   Later we watch them stumble through life's lessons, wishing to be able to make their decisions for them, already knowing the outcome of a mistake they are about to make. When we try to jump in and help, they resist and resent. But then there is that one sweet day when they let go of their pride, let go of their stranglehold on being in control, and they say, "Mom, Dad, I could use some help."

"I've just been waiting for you to ask," we might say.

That day in the bathroom, when my prayer hit God's ears, He simply said, "I've only been waiting for you to ask."

"*Though he falls, he shall not be utterly cast down, for the Lord grasps his hand in support and upholds him.*" -- Psalm 37:24

Chapter 19

Still Standing...

It is here.

Already I am up this morning. Already in the tub, enjoying a few moments of quiet before I race head first into this day.

It's bell ringer day.

This day of my last chemo, I look in the mirror and I see the evidence of the battle that has raged through my body, the path of destruction left behind.

Today looking back at me in the mirror is a fat old man. My head is no longer shiny bald. It seems that my hair is growing back in the order it left me. So the back and sides are covered in newborn baby-like hair, even hanging over my ears. The fun part is that it is NOT on the TOP of my head.

Yes, my hair is growing back but through some sad trick of chemo, as well as the dandelion fuzz on my head, the same fuzz has made its presence known on my face. I try not to pay it much mind. But what if it gets worse? Of course I googled it and from what others with the same experience have said, it should disappear on its own. But when? And what if it doesn't? Am I watching the beginnings of a man's beard that wasn't part of who I was before? My face is covered in a rash and is puffy from water retention and I pull up my pant legs to find cankles above my feet. I look in the mirror and notice my weight gain, even seeing it in my now oddly puffy armpits, never having noticed the beauty in their concave arch before all this. My belly is still bruised and dimpled from the shots and my constant hunger has turned me into a snack factory.

I look at myself and think, *Who are you?*

Preparing for Bell Ringer Day
January 28, 2011

These are the words I wrote the morning of my last chemotherapy, the day I had been working toward for so long.

It was a strange feeling knowing I was walking through the curtains of the lab area to have my port accessed for the last time. Giddy, excited, nervous, afraid, happy. I was all these things.

And as I stepped back through the sliding doors to join Kelley and my kids in the waiting room to wait until they called me back for my final treatment, my surprised eyes lit upon the smiling faces of my mother, my stepfather and my grandmother, who had kept secret their three-hour journey to be there with me on my special day. And then soon we were joined by my father and my circle was complete. The cornerstones of my existence present to hold me up, to carry me across the finish line.

My Outback buzzer buzzed and I entered the treatment center, climbed in the bed by the window in the pod to which I had been assigned, sat with my family as they took turns at my bedside and we watched the final drip, drip, drips of the IV, willing my body to make the most of it, so that I might never have to revisit a life such as this.

As the last bag of chemo hung from my IV pole, I looked up to see one of our favorite aids, Bridgette, and a gaggle of other nurses and aids heading toward my bed. Before I could get my mind to register what they were doing, Bridgette emptied a Styrofoam cup in my face. It seemed to go in slow motion as I tensed and waited for cold liquid to splash my face, my brain trying to speed up to the moment and understand simply WHY? But instead of the wet blast I was expecting, confetti, made of pink and yellow and white dots from a hole punch, rained down upon me as the group surrounded my hospital bed and applauded. They presented me with a certificate and a t-shirt that reads "CHEMOATHLON – I SURVIVED." Even in my groggy Benadryl state, it was something I will never forget.

I watched the monitor, counting down with its digital timer, staring at the chemo bag, following the last drop down the tube until it disappeared and the machine began to beep.

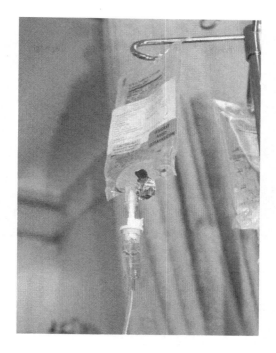

Fifteen times I had sat allowing a needle to pierce through my chest. Fifteen times I had allowed chemicals into my body that in a way gradually demolished the outer shell of who I was. Fifteen times I had shown up and accepted a treatment to course through my system, knowing the affects to come in the week to follow.

Fifteen times.

And now it was done.

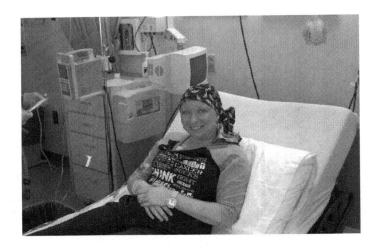

Surreal was the way it felt as the nurse removed the needle from my chest, freeing me from my chains. I didn't want to miss a thing, a moment, an emotion, but it was almost too much to grasp.

I stepped through the sliding doors into the waiting arms of my family. An amazing friend of mine, Kim, and her sister, Marie, were also waiting there for me with a balloon and pink teddy bear. Kim, who was there for a doctor's visit, had just recently completed her own chemotherapy treatments, and I had been blessed enough to be able to be there the day that HER hand rang the bell. Now, it was my turn.

The bell hung on the wall like a friend with an outstretched hand, ready and willing to ring loud and clear, to be my signal of victory over cancer. A steadfast marker, encouraging me through this battle, waiting patiently as I walked by each week, offering itself to sing the song of a job well done.

This was it. My hand went to the bell and my mind swam with images from the last few months.

The moment after I had broken the news to Kelley, as he knelt by our bed where I sat, tears streaming down both our faces, and his broken voice saying, "What do we do now?"

The emotional night we spent shaving my head and our midnight stroll after.

The endless sea of naps and aches.

The blood clots and the ambulance ride and the hospital stay.

Knowing how much life I'd missed out on in the last months while fighting this Ugly C-word...

How much of ME my kids had missed out on...

Knowing how exhausted, mentally and physically, Kelley must be...

Knowing how many tears had been shed in my honor...

How many sleepless nights my parents must have spent wondering "what if...."

I was lost in every thought, every moment, and my hand rang that bell a little harder with every one of them. I let go of the stranglehold I had on everything, on all of it. I let go. I rang the bell with ferocity, the rage in my heart screaming to cancer, "YOU DIDN'T BEAT ME! YOU DIDN'T BREAK ME! I'M STILL STANDING!"

When I finally stopped, I could feel the vibrations in my arm and the sound seemed to be reverberating off the walls and ceiling, and I turned into my mother's arms and sobbed.

Weeks before I had been standing in the waiting room when my nurse and friend, Michelle, had come through. She walked with a woman and stopped to introduce us saying she was new there. At the time, I assumed she meant she was going to be working there and that Michelle was showing her around. Moments later though, I saw her sitting in the waiting room with a couple I thought must be her mother and father. As they sat together, tears flowed down her face as the couple whispered encouraging words to her. This had haunted me and played over and over in my mind since that day. I wish I had been brave enough to not worry about overstepping my bounds and had sat with her and put my arms around her and told her it was all going to be ok. But I didn't know her situation. I had no way of knowing if her diagnosis was worse than mine. Was she crying because she was afraid of the unknown like I had been? Or was chemo all there was left for her to try? If I told her it was all going to be ok, would that have been a lie? In the end I did nothing, the pull of my own appointment dragging me from the waiting area, leaving me with tugged heart strings for a woman I didn't know.

Now, at the very moment I announced the completion of my own chemotherapy to every heart on the 7th floor, this woman came rounding the corner. Here we were, face to face after all this time. I could see it register in her face why I was standing there, and her voice seemed to almost beg as she said, "Are you done?"

"Yes," I said. And she fell into my arms, weeping.

God's timing. I believe it was God's timing that put me in the presence of this woman that very first day. God that let her weigh on my heart. God that already had a plan in place for us to meet again at a moment that would heal us both. For me to be able to hug her and tell her it would be all right. For her to put her arms around me and see that it really would.

In the beginning when I first saw the bell and the sign, I pictured the day my children would watch me ring the bell. It was to be a symbolic gesture, as a graduate switches his tassel from one side to the other after crossing that stage, a signal to my children that this is done. I had chased the monster away.

I never imagined, though how empowering it would be for me. I will forever cherish the feeling of strength that washed over me as I hung on that bell with all my might, in the loving circle of my family, sounding the trumpets that declared victory over this invisible opponent, shouting to the rooftops that my life was worth it, the fight was worth it...

And it was true.

It WAS one of those moments.

And we ALL smiled.

Chapter 20

Fight Like Heck...

I was three years old when my parents moved us to Bernie, Missouri. I was five when I started kindergarten here. Eighteen when I graduated from its high school. Nineteen when Kelley and I were married at the Bernie United Methodist Church. Twenty-one and twenty-six when I brought my babies here to claim this town as their own. Thirty-five when, in the quiet subdivision I live in right past the city limit sign, I received the news that I had cancer. Bernie holds the memories of my entire life, the characters in my story are the people I know by name that live in the houses dotting every street in this town. No visit to the post office or the Dollar Store or the grocery store or simple drive through town ever happens without me seeing someone I know.

I pick sticker burrs out of my yard and hold in my hand like bouquets of flowers. Crop dusters zoom in the air over the fields close to my home, sounding like they might touch my roof at any minute and spray defoliant that makes me sneeze. When the wind blows through the dry fields, the dust flies like a storm in the desert. The mosquitos make it impossible here to be outside after sunset during the summer without a solid coating of bug spray and even then I think that just makes them feistier.

But here I know what it's like to ride around on gravel roads and never meet another car. From my home on a night in early summer, I can hear the cheers from the little league baseball games. On the 4th of July I can watch the dance of light in the open sky above the fields from the fireworks show in the neighboring town, just by sitting in my own backyard. In the fall, the townspeople gather in the park for the Fall Fest, eating funnel cakes and hamburgers and hotdogs, watching the beauty pageant and shopping for crafts, all the while visiting with the people whose lives intertwine with their own.

The trials and tribulations and the joys and wonders of each of the people in a small town like this are suffered and celebrated together. The ups and downs of my own life are a part of the ups and downs of theirs.

So I am not sure why I was overwhelmed by the outpouring of love I received from a community such as this when my own cancer came to town.

It was the day after my very last chemotherapy, Bell Ringer Day, that was chosen by my friends and family as the day for Fight Like Heck for Beck. I think out of the entire story I have told so far, this is the hardest chapter for me to write. It is rare for me to be fresh out of words but about this I am still speechless. Words fail me, and I find it hard to describe this special night in my life.

My longtime friend, Nicole, came up with the idea for a benefit for Kelley and I and our kids to help with the outstanding bills that come with any medical diagnosis, much less a diagnosis of cancer. Medical bills, gas, meals, hotel stays, and the day to day bills already at home waiting to be paid with purse strings tightened already by the fact that suddenly our home had gone from a two income family to one.

I was so nervous to go to the benefit. Already I had no idea how to thank them all for the hard work they had put in just to plan it. How was I to react or thank them once I was there and I saw what their hard work had all been about?

Nicole was joined by a group of my close friends that took time out of their already busy lives, gathering donations for the event from the community and towns close by. Donations of money and gift certificates for services, items from businesses for the live and silent auctions, and baked goods for the bake sale. Marcus Norden, a fellow survivor who battled leukemia, stood with Kelley late through the night and again in the early morning hours, smoking Boston butts for the barbecue sandwiches they would sell along with the sodas and chips that were donated.

They had awesome t-shirts made with a logo of "Fight Like Heck for Beck" worn by the team of people who put this event together and that they sold at the door. When I entered the room that evening already buzzing with activity, I was led to the table at the front that welcomed the guests. The table covered in a pink table cloth with a sign sporting the words *Operation Healthy Hooters* from the slogan printed on the pink and white marbled rubber wrist bands sold after my diagnosis, also held a 16 x 20 black and white print of me in all my bald-headed glory, and behind it the smiling faces of Summer, Nicole, and Krystal. Tables set up in the middle of the room were covered in white table cloths while pink and white balloons floated in clusters above them.

Silent and live auctions raised money with items such as a Vera Bradley purse in the print designated to raise money for breast cancer research, a kitchen table and a bench made by the loving hands of my mother from her primitive furniture business White House Creations; and there were birdfeeders, work boots, Cardinals tickets, gift certificates to area restaurants, a car cleaning kit, car seat covers, candles, and a set of screwdrivers. If you could think of it, it was there for the bidding.

And as if all that wasn't enough, we were able to spend the night listening to the sweet voice of Rebekah Northern, rocking with the band 100 Proof, mesmerized by the soulful sounds of Dub Pierce and the country in us let loose to the songs of my cousin, rising star Justin Heskett. I smiled as I watched little ones boogie on the dance floor, as I slow danced with my husband to the beat of a slow tune, as I listened to the giggles of the girls holding hands chanting, "Red rover, red rover send Mallory right over!"

At the end of the night, a slideshow was played set to the songs "Pink Warrior" by Candy Coburn and "I Am Not My Hair" sang by India Arie and Pink. The slideshow a surprise collection of the photos taken by Julie Dodd, showing me bald but fighting, vulnerable yet strong; the pictures themselves telling a story that needed no words. It was emotional to see myself in that light, to see what those moments in battle might look like from the outside looking in. And as the video ended, all who were there to see it rose to their feet and gave me a standing ovation.

That night, a town full of people who love me, a community of some who don't even know me, a room full of the people who make up who I am, gathered together to lend their hearts and hands to make what we were going through easier, to let me see with my own eyes what I already knew in my heart, that they had been standing alongside me the whole time, cheering me on, and celebrating the victory with me that was already mine.

When it was all said and done, when the music stopped, when the decorations were pulled down, the tables and chairs put back in their rightful places, the guest list contained the names of over 300 people who had attended "Fight Like Heck for Beck."

And the fruits of the labor of love my precious friends worked so hard on totaled over $10,000.

Now maybe you can understand why words about this fail me. I have found words to tell here about that night but I close knowing they weren't the right ones. No words could ever paint the picture of such a perfect night full of love and celebration. No words could possibly do it justice; no thank you's could ever be enough.

The battle is not over for me, the next phase soon to begin. But my spirit has been refreshed, the strength to fight renewed. And though the fight is mine, I have seen with my own eyes that I am not alone. Because the place I call home fights like heck with me.

Chapter 21

No place like home...

How am I supposed to do this? It's Sunday morning. Today is the day that Kelley and I head to St. Louis. He will come home on Wednesday. And for six weeks....I won't.

Kelley has been gone on business trips or hunting trips before, never for more than a few days here or there. I have spent the night away from home on occasion. My annual shopping trip I took to Paducah with my friend, Robin, or a sleepover at a former teacher's house with my "Ya Ya" sisters (a group of my best friends that I graduated with). One night, maybe two. Never a week, never a month, NEVER six weeks. My place is right here at home.

This is another part of my journey I have raced at blindly. I want it done. I want this behind us. Although I was here in this house with my husband and children for the most part, it feels like chemo robbed me of the last four months. Oh, I made it trick or treating even though I thought I would miss it. I made it to Thanksgiving dinner after doing chemo the day before. I had chemo on Christmas Eve Eve and New Years Eve Eve and was home to enjoy the holidays with my family. Kelley's birthday was spent on the road taking me for treatment, and I remember him being excited that his birthday fell on a day that we could spend together. I made it to all the big stuff I was so afraid in the beginning that I would miss. Yet, how many things did I miss right here at home?

We made it through the chemo, through days when instead of me taking care of my family, they took care of me. And now this. Because insurance can be a funny thing and because the care at Siteman is so phenomenal, I decided to have my radiation treatments done in St. Louis. Radiation is every day, five days a week, for six weeks. Although we were a bit unsure at first of what the right decision was for us on where to do my treatments, once we met my radiation oncologist in St. Louis, we knew this was the best for me. This has been a long road for not only me but for Kelley and the kids and for my family and friends. So although this will take me far from home, I'll do it for them because I love them all so much. I want to do this as right as I can the first time so we never have to look back and wonder if we had gone as big as we could go. This is the right thing for me. I know it. It doesn't make it easy.

So how do I go in there and wake my babies up this morning? What do I say? They need to see me strong and unwavering. Instead I am crushed that I must leave them.

If I can just get through this day. As I write this, it seems impossible.

It was just about a couple of years ago that I went to have dinner with some of my friends I graduated with. I was only going maybe 15 minutes away to the neighboring town, but for some reason, Mal did NOT want me to go. I suppose it was because I rarely go anywhere without them. I will never forget though when she came up to me before I left and gave me a little square of paper, a tiny bit larger than a postage stamp. It read, "I will miss you. 293-xxxx." She had written our home phone number on there like I might forget it.

I was home that night in about an hour and a half and to this day that piece of paper is in my wallet. In case I ever need to call home.

Mallory, who is ten, had an intramural volleyball game yesterday. Her team lost but to be honest, I didn't notice. When I arrived at the game and was looking for a seat, I noticed a little boy notice me. He stared at me in awe, and I assumed it was my head scarf that had him enamored. I watched him point me out to his friend. He waved to me. We made a little secret wave between us where we flicked our thumbs and forefingers at one another. I wasn't sure why, but he did it and I copied and it seemed like fun. He couldn't keep his eyes off me and after a while, he began to speak to me but I couldn't quite make out the words. Whatever it was he would say it and then wave and wave. And then I was able to read his lips. He was saying, "Hi Pirate!"

And with my head scarf and hoop earrings, that is exactly what I looked like. To him I must have been a celebrity, one of the Wiggles or the captain's wife on "SpongeBob." It's moments like that I will treasure. Get it? Pirate...treasure...? Anyhoo...

I sat by my son through the game and feasted with him on popcorn and nachos, a breakfast of champions. I watched my beautiful daughter get all her serves over. I marveled at how grown up she looked, beginning to look more like a teenager than a 10-year old.

When the game was over, she shuffled up to us. For the first time I saw her daddy's competitive nature in her face.

"What's wrong, Pook?" Kelley asked using the special nickname he has for her.

"We lost," she answered.

"That's ok!" we both told her. "You played so well. You got all your serves over and you called the ball just like you were supposed to."

She went for snacks and when she returned, it was only me on the bench.

"I didn't want to lose today," she said.

"Well, honey, it's all right. You get to play again next weekend!"

And with tears in her eyes she said, "I didn't want to lose today because this is the last game you're going to get to see me play and I wanted you to see me win."

Words failed me.

She sat down beside me and I pulled her close and fought the tears that threatened to fall, because I knew I was hanging on by a thread and when the dam broke, it wasn't going to stop.

Before I could muster up any encouraging words though, her friends came up and said her coach wanted her down at the other side of the gym to cheer for the 5th and 6th grade team. I suppose her friend saw it in her eyes that something was wrong but she asked no questions. They simply walked away, holding hands. Their teenage appearance revealed as just a facade.

These are the times that make me want to shout, that make me ask, "Why does it have to be so hard? Haven't we already been through enough?" But there would be no answer, no satisfactory one at least. The fight would still be mine to finish, the outcome the same.

So now here we are. I have put it off as long as I can.

Good morning. Wake up so I can tell you goodbye.

Chapter 22

At the beginning again...

Here I am once again. In a waiting room, in a gown, this one open in the back. It's February 21, day one of radiation and I'm waiting my turn.

Kelley asked me if I was scared. "A little bit. Fear of the unknown," I said.

Now as I'm only minutes away now instead of months or weeks or days, I just want to get it done. I want it over. I've been through surgery and chemo and shots and things that burned and hurt and things that made me sleepy and nauseous. So I hate to assume too much, but I don't expect today's treatment specifically to be too bad.

But what if it is? That's where my head is. Today, radiation is the unknown, and yes I'm a bit afraid.

And irritated. I've felt anger for the first time really in the last couple of days. I suppose the anger comes from "momma bear syndrome." The fact that this whole cancer mess is taking me from my kids for 6 weeks and that that hurts them, well, that got my hackles up. And then that makes me take it a bit further. I'm sick of being poked and prodded, of taking medicines or getting IVs pumped in me. I'm tired of being away from home. I'm tired of not having hair and of being so much bigger than usual. Sigh.

But I can be tired of it all I want and it doesn't change things. I still have radiation to do, and I'll do it every day to make sure I come out the winner on this thing.

They'll call my name any minute now. Almost my turn. Actually, I am kind of excited that they might take these durn pieces of tape off of me that they've placed everywhere that itch me so bad.

Yesterday, Kelley and I drove up here and moved me in to Hope Lodge, only a couple of streets over from the hospital. Sponsored by the American Cancer Society, Hope Lodge gives patients that live over 50 miles away a place to stay while they are getting treatment done.

I never went away to college, but I feel like I'm getting my opportunity to experience dorm living. I have my own room with two twin beds and my own bathroom. Each room has its own heating/cooling system and I am ecstatic! With these hot flashes I've been experiencing... wait... power surges, Kelley calls them, I have been able to turn the room into an iceberg and I have slept like a champ!

I am not allowed food or drink inside my room. So although that sends a streak of panic through me, I am looking forward to all the pounds I will surely lose when I am not able to stuff a cookie in my mouth at every commercial. I CAN have water in my room so that will be another added bonus in the healthy new Beck I am hoping leaves here in 6 weeks.

And there's a curfew. 11:00-7:00 the alarm system is turned on and there is no leaving or getting in unless it's an emergency. Well, I don't WANT to go anywhere in the middle of the night, and I seriously doubt I'll be going anywhere that is going to keep me out late enough to miss curfew. But I'll admit, at 35 years old, it feels strange to have rules again.

But the end all be all of travesties, the one thing that could possibly be worse than no food or drink in my room...there is no Wi-Fi. Oh have mercy on me. How giddy I was when out in front of the building I happened to hone in on someone's connection. I don't know if that's illegal or not and on top of that I'll be danged if I suddenly couldn't think of anything I needed Wi-Fi for at the moment. But I'm relieved none the less.

So I am settling in to my new home and now here we

are... at the beginning again. This time though, at the beginning of the last big step. Time to get my game face on. After today, only 29 more treatments to go!

Chapter 23

How to train your wife…

Kelley is still with me. Yesterday he drove me here to radiation. Today we tried out the shuttle system provided by Barnes. Here in the city, it is cold today. 33 degrees as we sat outside anxiously awaiting the arrival of the 12:50 bus. The schedule posted says that the shuttle stops outside every day every two hours starting at 7:00. 7:00, 8:50, 10:50, 12:50, 2:50, 4:50, 6:50. However, as I sat and shivered and watched my breath in the cold air, 12:50 came and the bus did not. It gave us plenty of time though for Kelley to start my training.

Before we even left home, he found a way to get me some mace. So today, knowing he is leaving me tomorrow, he has begun to plot out my every day safety plan.

My mace goes on the table by the door. "This is the first thing you lay down when you walk into this room and the last thing you pick up when you leave it." Yes, sir. So today when it was time to leave, it began.

How to Train Your Wife...

"Ok, you're about to walk out the door. What are you gonna do?" he began.

"Get my mace," I said channeling the snotty teenage girl that still lives within me.

"And then what are you going to do?"

"Leave."

"No, you're going to..." he prompted, waiting for me to spout the correct answer. When it didn't come, he finished. "You're going to put it in the front pocket of your hoodie."

"That's what I said."

"No, it's not," he corrected. "Then what are you going

to do?"

"Leave."

"Where's your hand going to go?" he asked, his loss of patience beginning to show in the new octave his voice was taking.

"In my pocket..." I answered. But then unable to fight the urge, finished with "And the other one is giving the peace sign."

"Your HAND is going to go on the can of MACE until you get where you are going!" he growled. I think I just got grounded.

Down in front of the building as we sat on the bench, well, as I sat on the bench and he stood, when the first person walked by on the sidewalk, I watched Kelley's eyes go directly to my hoodie pocket. I passed the test because my hand sat snugly wrapped around the can, finger on the trigger.

The bus came at a little after 1:00 and we hopped on. Another first and another unknown I am glad to have behind me. Soon I'll be a pro, hopping on the bus and saying *Hey* to the driver and the others I recognize from previous trips.

The problem today is that the bus runs at Hope Lodge again at 2:50 and not again until 4:50. The bus runs its regular route every twenty minutes but will bypass Hope Lodge until its scheduled time. Any other day I think it would be no big deal and I would have plenty of time to get back on the 2:50, but on Tuesdays, I have to see the doctor after treatment and they just came back and told me that the machine is getting some maintenance done and it will be a little bit. Hmmmmmmmmm....I'm not making the 2:50 drop off.

So, tomorrow I think I will have Kelley accompany me as I try some city driving and skip the bus ride.

And for some reason I'm thinking tomorrow's episode of "How to Train Your Wife" is going to end with me in a timeout with my nose in the corner or Kelley with a face full of mace. How soon he forgets I keep it in my hoodie pocket.

Chapter 24

Letting it all hang out...

I am resigned to uncomfortable situations at this point. I mean, come on, it was BREAST cancer. Maybe when you think of me and my breast cancer, you picture me and my bald head or me hooked up to an IV pole. In reality, me and my breast cancer translates into me spending much of the last months baring my breast to complete strangers.

First, there was the exam where my gynecologist found the lump during the breast exam of my Pap smear. Then after finding the lump, she sent me for a mammogram and ultrasound. Oh, now there's part of the story I haven't put down for posterity yet. Stay with me. This is the part of the book where I do some flashback scenes.

This whole experience has been unchartered territory for me and at the young age of 35, a mammogram was no different. All I had ever heard about a mammogram was that it was painful. I could only imagine having any of your parts smushed would be uncomfortable. But I figured I was tough and could handle it. And maybe whoever had told me it was painful had just gotten a bad machine or a new technician that didn't know what they were doing.

One way or the other, I really didn't allow myself to focus on it. I expected it all to be a fearful moment in this story of me and that in a couple of days it would all be in the past, the anticipation and anxiety of it all a waste of a few days, a skip in my record.

So, ready...set...go.

Kelley sat in the waiting room that day and waited patiently, unbeknownst to either of us that this would be the first of about a million times in his all too near future that he would take up residence in a room much like this. I gowned up and rattled nervously to the technician, my intention to come off blasé and in control of the situation. So far this tactic has still never been successful, resulting in almost every technician, nurse or doctor that I have encountered at some point, I'm sure, thinking that I must be off my rocker a bit.

"Ok," began the tech "what brings you here today?"

"Well, I have a spot on my right side that they are concerned about," I told her.

"And did you find this yourself?" she asked as she looked through my chart.

Oh the guilt. I wanted to hang my head. I SHOULD have been doing my own self exams. But I hadn't been. There. The truth is out. Throughout our whole marriage Kelley had always asked me, "Have you been checking yourself lately?" and maybe it was a mental eye roll he received from me and not one that he ever noticed, but nonetheless, it was there.

Yeah Yeah Yeah. Breast cancer. It could happen. So could an earthquake. We live on the New Madrid fault. Tornadoes. We live in Missouri. The bird flu. Those dumb things are everywhere.

But now, there was a lump in my breast and I hadn't been doing my self exams. There was a lump in my very own breast and I didn't even know about it. It took a stranger feeling me up to find it.

"No, my gynecologist found it during my yearly Pap smear. She said it was probably just a fluid-filled cyst but thought we should get it checked out," I confessed.

"Sure. Sure. Ok, is there any breast cancer that runs in your family? Any cancer at all?"

"No breast cancer at all," I said proudly. "My mother's father died of lung cancer many, many years ago but that's it."

"Ok, good. What about caffeine? Do you drink a lot of tea or sodas?"

"YES!" I said way too adamantly. "Lots of Diet Pepsi! I LOVE Diet Pepsi." I suppose my fears were trying to surface, and I was willing them away with my new confessions of caffeine addiction. This guilty pleasure, a known cause of fibroid cysts, that was sure to be the culprit of this lump. Darn you, you carbonated thirst quencher. Darn you!

Questioning finished, she reclined my chair, opened my gown and did a breast exam. I guided her to the general direction of the lump and began my first of many unsuccessful attempts to read the reactions of my examiners.

"Ok, I'm going to sit you up now and have you come over here," she said. "Drop your gown off your right side and step up to the machine."

First, let me explain that God designed me with a small chest. And as disappointing as that in itself is, He also made one side obviously smaller than the other. Now this is a fairly normal thing for women but, to me, mine seemed a little more noticeable than most. It is necessary to divulge this bit of information so that I can explain this next part of the story.

It was at this point that a nervous compulsion led me to say the dumbest thing.

"Now, this is my little one. So I don't know that it will actually fit into your machine."

To my dismay, my attempt at comic relief BACKFIRED. Meant to lighten the mood, I think she took it as a CHALLENGE.

"Oh, I'll get it in there," she said.

Oh no. What had I done? The cards had been dealt. The dye had been cast. I had set wheels in motion and it was TOO late!

I stepped forward, placing my little guy on a small "shelf" in front of me. I started taking in my surroundings, trying to predict what was going to happen next. She rattled with settings and guided me forward more, my head turned as far as it would go to the left.

And then she began to bring down the top plate,

enclosing it over my right breast.

My mind tried to work it out, the physics of it all. The machine was surely made for regular-sized breasts and this one in question was hardly regular sized. So when the machine closed, it wouldn't be near as tight or painful as on say a *normal*-sized chest.

Except for that I was wrong.

She closed the top plate down over my breast and I took a deep breath. It was tight. There was a lot of pressure. I didn't like it but I was OK. I braced myself and just waited for her to push the button and take the picture or whatever it is they do at a mammogram.

Instead, she grabbed the side of my breast and pushed it farther into the machine. She closed the plates some more. She grabbed more flesh and tucked it in, closing the machine more. At this point I think she began moving my back fat over to the side, determined to come out the winner on this thing.

With my head turned away from her, I couldn't see what she was actually doing. But I was envisioning her intently working on getting this little guy in the machine, pressing every piece of meat she could get a hold of, tongue stuck out to the side in concentration, turning to the side to use her own body mass to press mine into this contraption.

Even though I thought there was NO way this vice could possibly clamp any tighter on my little bump, it did, and when she finally got me in place and she stepped back, all I could do was hold my breath and scrunch up my face to work through the discomfort – no, the pain.

I feel a little guilty describing this experience as honestly as I am. I don't want to discourage anyone from going and getting a mammogram. And granted, I probably went in there a little sore already because honestly, after being told I had a lump, I couldn't help but check repeatedly to see if it had by any chance gone away on its own. Pretending though that it was a relaxing experience and not painful wouldn't benefit anyone, and plus I want everyone to know I was a big girl about it.

She released me from my hold, and I stepped back relieved only to watch this machine turn from a horizontal position to a diagonal one and my irrational mind, muddled and surely now scarred, pictured the plates twisting like that while my chest was still in it. Of course that didn't happen but just the idea made me a little woozy.

I honestly can't remember how many times she closed the squisher over my right side, but I just remember the process taking my breath away, and then I remember her telling me to hold my breath for the picture when I had already BEEN holding my breath because I had a body part in a vice grip.

I imagined I was turning blue from lack of oxygen and then had the horrible thought of me passing out while still clamped into this machine and just hanging there unconscious by my boob.

When it was over, I remember sitting down beside Kelley in the waiting room, still in my gown.

"How was it, Momma?" he asked. "You ok?

With a smile plastered on my face for the benefit of anyone watching, I answered him.

"That was awful," I said cheerily. "I am NEVER doing that again."

"Ok, Rebecca," the receptionist said. "We're going to have you go down the hall for your ultrasound."

Arriving at another waiting room for Kelley to enjoy, I signed my name and had a seat, and in just moments they called my name.

After suffering through the mammogram and not really having time to mentally work through and block out this traumatic event, I followed a technician back into a dimly lit room. She directed me to lie down and open my gown.

"Ok, I'm going to put some of this gel on you. It should be nice and warm," she said.

She gave the bottle a squeeze and nothing. So she gave it a sharp shake and another squeeze. The bottle rattled with airy noise, a sound that I'm sure causes hilarity to ensue all over the world, and spattered up my neck and across my face.

"Oh my gosh! I'm so sorry," she said, attempting to wipe the out of control gel off my chin.

"Yeah, it's fine. Don't worry!" I said, mentally shaking my head and thinking, *Oh, so the whole DAY is going to be like this.*

She placed the wand over my breast, swirling and pressing it in a pattern of concentric circles. I watched the screen, tickled there was somewhere to focus my eyes while yet another person was up close and personal with a body part I am intended to keep covered. I remember thinking what I was seeing to me resembled diagrams in my old science books where they described the different layers of the earth, the crust and the mantle. And then she got to the lump.

When I was pregnant and I had an ultrasound done, a black circle appeared on the screen, a fluid filled sack that held in it a tiny white smudge, my baby.

So I was surprised that when she ran the wand over the lump in my breast, a dark shadowy shape appeared.

"You know," I remember saying out loud, "you'd expect that to look like a circle, wouldn't ya? But it doesn't. Looks more like a triangle to me."

Insert uncomfortable silence here.

Eventually she continued her circular path on the rest of my breast but made her way back to the lump. The shadowy figure was there again, the edges undefined and cloudy.

"Does it hurt at all?" she asked.

"Well, it's sore now because I just had it in a machine that squashed it flat. But other than that, no, it doesn't hurt at all." My breasts have always been tender but that particular spot never hurt until my doctor found it, and I couldn't help but feel it all the time and made it sore. She nodded her head quietly as she continued the ultrasound.

"Hang on just a second, " she said after a few minutes, and she departed behind the curtain, returning with a man. I had the distinct feeling that he was a superior of some kind, and I felt like I had cracked the code.

Ohhhhh, she must be NEW. She's in TRAINING. She's never done a breast exam before and surely not on a LUMP. And that must be why it looked dark and shadowy on the screen. She had the settings wrong. Or she'd just never seen a fibroid cyst before. Well, when you look at it like that, I was glad I came, glad to help and be a learning experience for her.

She sat back down at her seat and he stood behind her. And there I was, lying on the bed with my stuff hanging out, pretending like it didn't feel weird to have a strange man in there as I lay there exposed.

They bantered back and forth about this setting and that, him seeming to direct her from his position. Did you do this or that?

"Do you know where it is?" he asked me, referring to the location of the lump.

The grip on my modesty at this point tortured and worn thin, my inhibitions gone, I said, "Yeah, it's right here. You can feel it," and fell short of grabbing his hand so he could feel it himself. I just wanted it over. I couldn't take much more. I was on overload.

"Here, let me sit there," he told the tech and took her seat and the wand, again pressing and swirling on the lump.

"And does it hurt?" he asked.

"No, not at all," I answered, exhausted by the whole thing.

"Ok," he finally said. "You're all done." He handed me a towel so I could wipe off the ultrasound gel.

"Oh. Ok, thanks." I said, sitting up.

They left me alone behind the drawn curtain to change out of the gown. My mind was spinning so fast. I couldn't think about it or make sense of it just yet. I just needed to get out of there first. I smiled at them and thanked them again as I came out from behind the curtain and passed them on the way out of the room.

"Good luck," he said.

What did he just say?

Did he just say *Good luck*? I wanted to turn around and say, *What the heck did you mean by that?*

The mammogram lady had passed me in the hall with a good luck, a wink and a knowing smile. I was comforted by her "code" saying everything was fine.

Now this man just said *Good luck* in a way that made me feel not so warm and fuzzy.

It was surely nothing but a fibroid cyst and the mammogram and ultrasound were now over. I had almost relaxed and breathed a sigh of relief knowing that the ordeal was behind me, and now at the last second he throws in a *Good Luck*!

I rounded the corner and found Kelley.

"Are you ready?" I said, with an irritated tone already walking away, expecting him to follow right behind me.

"What'd they say?" he asked, trying to catch up with me.

"Good luck. Now take me home."

It was only the next day that the call came. I remember sitting at my desk at work, thankfully being between clients, so I was able to have a private moment when the nurse told me the mammogram and ultrasound had come back *suspicious* and that I needed to schedule a biopsy.

So there's the story of the beginning, the firsts of many examinations, the start of a journey where Beck starts letting it all hang out.

Chapter 25

Kudos...

A cyst. A mammogram. An ultrasound. All these things were events that definitely sparked some anxiety but seemed to be just things I certainly dreaded but that were necessary to rule out that anything was awry. I mentally approached them as best I could, looking at them as I might look at tests done to rule out a bladder infection or a kidney stone.

But a biopsy. That word is frightening. That word is serious and caused my mind to retreat a little, to huddle in my shell a bit until forced to deal.

Mammogram and ultrasound pictures and a CD in hand for the surgeon I was to see, I waited patiently and sweetly oblivious to what this particular appointment would hold or lead to.

I remember sitting in the waiting room for a very long time because the doctor I was seeing was held up in surgery. Myself, Kelley, my mother, step father, grandmother, my children and my friend, Robin sat together, visiting and laughing as we passed the time.

"Mom, you should tell Robin the story about the trivia question you answered the other day," I said, giggling as she ducked her head and rolled her pretty eyes.

A few weeks before, she and my stepfather had gone to eat fish at a nearby restaurant. Hanging on the wall was a sign that had trivia questions that crawled by on its screen. The question she read was *How deep is the water during a water polo match?* Evidently she thought about it really hard and then very thoughtfully reasoned OUT LOUD "Well, I want to say eight feet but then the horses would drown! So I'll say six."

According to the story, after catching his breath from laughter, Steve red-faced said, "Dot, there are no horses in water polo."

After mom told the story, we sat in the waiting room and laughed until we cried. I'm sure the receptionist and other people in the waiting room were definitely ready for the doctor to show up so they could get us out of there.

When they did call my name, Kelley and I followed the nurse back to another room, where I was instructed again to disrobe above the waist and put on a gown. Soon the nurse practitioner came in and introduced herself. We discussed a mutual friend and after a bit of small talk she asked me to lie back on the table. Again I opened my gown for another stranger to examine me.

"And who found this lump?" she asked.

"My gynecologist found it during my yearly pap," I said shaking off the urge to rattle about caffeine and my guilt for not finding the spot myself.

She exited the room and soon returned with the actual doctor I was there to see. As this fairly young man examined me, my mind wandered to Kelley, and it occurred to me that this was the first time he'd been present when I had an examination done. I wondered how it made him feel, whether or not it made him uncomfortable. Where was his head at that moment? Were the words *get your hands off my wife* running through his mind? Or was he glad that we had finally reached the moment that the surgeon we'd been waiting to see was to do his job?

"Who found this lump?" the doctor asked as he pressed the area in question.

"My gynecologist," I answered.

"There's definitely something here. It's small though. Kudos to your doctor for finding it," and almost as quickly as he had appeared, he was gone.

"Ok," said the nurse practitioner. "We're going to go take a look at your films and the CD of the ultrasound and then we'll go from there. Worst case scenario, we'll have you go down the hall here for an ultrasound-guided needle biopsy. But that's worst case scenario. I'll be back as soon as I can."

I could almost breathe easier. This was it. Finally. This was the extreme in the list of doctors I'd had to see. We were at the top of the chain, and this was the moment that the experts dismissed it as nothing to worry about and we could put this whole thing behind us, and I could run across the street to the mall for some retail therapy. I was tightly wound and emotionally exhausted. I'd held it together but I was totally over it and ready to move on.

There was a knock at the door and the nurse practitioner re-entered.

"Rebecca, we're going to have you come down the hall here for a biopsy. If you'll just come this way."

Wait.

Worst case scenario.

You just said it.

I numbly followed behind her around the corner and down a very short hallway where another nurse waited.

What did this mean?

Game face. Game face.

The nurse explained it would be a few minutes as they set up and asked Kelley if there was anyone in the waiting room with us he needed to update.

"Do you want me to go get your Mom?" Kelley asked me.

"No, just go let them know what's going on. I'm fine."

The master of happy faces and small talk, I chit chatted with the nurse until Kelley returned.

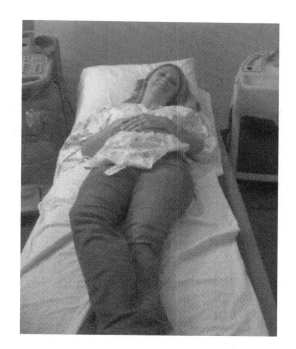

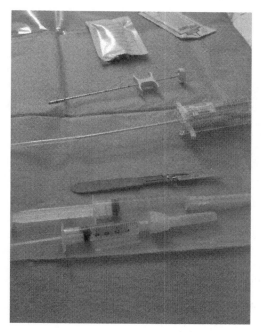

On a tray, the nurse laid out all the tools to be used for the biopsy, and Kelley studied them wide-eyed, asking questions about the procedure, while I tried to seem nonchalant and perfectly in control of the whole situation.

It wasn't long before we were joined by the radiologist who would be doing the actual biopsy. Both he and the nurse were so sweet and comforting and put us at ease by keeping us informed about everything they were doing.

The procedure started with the radiologist numbing the area and then making an incision with a scalpel that looked to me more like an X-acto knife from art class. He then inserted a syringe into the incision and with the nurse holding the ultrasound wand on my breast, we were able to see the needle going through the tissue numbing the area of the mass itself. How I was able to watch and not pass out is beyond me.

It was the next step though that they advised me not to watch. In layman's terms, of course, I'll describe this next piece of equipment as a needle with a trigger. Kelley watched as the radiologist inserted a large gage needle, almost "burying it" he said, into my breast. He inserted it into the mass itself and he described the procedure as a little like "coring an apple." Once he had it in place and pulled the trigger, he was able to retrieve a sample of the mass. This sample was then placed in a specimen cup to be sent off for testing. Kelley took a picture of the sample as well as the tray of instruments, for bragging rights of course. Little did we know that he was capturing a picture of the cancer that we hadn't been introduced to yet.

After the sample was taken, the doctor then used another needle-like piece to place a titanium marker in the mass so that the area could be easily found and noted in any future mammograms or tests. The nurse read my mind and was quick to tell us, "No, you won't set off any metal detectors at the airport." I was definitely relieved because I imagine that would have led to one heck of a strip search.

Then at this point, as if I hadn't already been through enough, they sent me down the hall for another mammogram. And my thoughts ran to the fact that they had just made an incision in my breast and now they wanted to mash it flat again. What was going to keep my guts from coming out? Ridiculous deep thought but I was in a weirdly mental overloaded place. This mammogram, however, was only slightly uncomfortable though, even pleasant compared to my last.

I left the office, numb and bandaged and already blocking out the whole mess. While at the appointment, my iPhone locked up and because no one would dare cross me at this point, I instructed Kelley to take me immediately to the phone place for technical assistance. I needed an outlet, something different to focus my energy on, fighting the feelings of panic and fear the appointment had stirred. I remember sitting at the store, my nerves at a breaking point, starved and sweating, pieces of the last few hours pecking at my mind and my resolve like pebbles flying at a pane of glass, threatening to shatter any minute. What had just happened?

"Kudos to your doctor for finding this," the surgeon had said.

And six days later, when I met with another surgeon, this time in St. Louis, and she felt the lump for the first time during her initial exam, remarkably she too said the words, "Kudos to your doctor for finding this."

Two separate surgeons giving kudos (defined in the dictionary as *praise for an achievement*) to another doctor for finding a lump in my breast. What does that mean? It stood out to me then and always stayed in the back of my mind.

I almost didn't go to the gynecologist that day. I don't remember my reasoning for wanting to reschedule. But I didn't. I went anyway.

There's no history of breast cancer, or any cancer really, in my family. So honestly I probably never would have thought to look or found it myself until it was too late.

My doctor found the lump even when there had been no suspicion, no pain. She found a lump so small that the surgeons I saw afterward gave her a nod of respect by giving her kudos.

My cancer was stage ONE.

Dr. Jennifer Waller saved my life.

I've said before I do not understand God's plan. But it's times in my life like this that I can see His fingerprints all over it.

We could call it coincidence.

We could call it luck.

But I won't.

"Trust God from the bottom of your heart; don't try to figure out everything on your own. Listen for God's voice in everything you do, everywhere you go; He's the one who will keep you on track."

---Proverbs 3:5-6

Don't try to figure it out, it says. Just listen for His voice.

If I'd been going to a different doctor, would they have found it?

What would have happened if I hadn't gone that day for my Pap smear, if I'd rescheduled it like I had considered?

What would have happened if some little distraction had thrown her off and she had missed the lump?

The answers to the *what if's* just don't matter. But the *what if's* certainly tell a story, don't they?

"For I know the plans I have for you – [this is] the Lord's declaration – "plans for [your] welfare, not for disaster, to give you a future and a hope."

---Jeremiah 29:11 Holman CSB

So to God I give praise and glory for the plan He had laid out for me, for the wheels He set in motion to give me life and hope.

Kudos, Father. Kudos.

Chapter 26

Obladi Oblada…

After receiving the news that the lump in my breast was cancer, the next step was to meet with a surgeon to discuss where we would go from there. I remember making a call to a doctor's office and getting an answering service. I left a message and was satisfied to wait. The strain and stress and shock of it all seemed to cause me to shut down. As the wife, as the mommy, I have always been the one in control of all situations, making calls, making appointments, but the merry-go-round that was my mind wouldn't stop spinning and I just wanted off. My head was pounding from crying. I was mentally and physically exhausted and my swollen eyes had no choice but to close for a respite from my new reality.

When I awoke, I found Kelley talking on the phone. While I was sleeping, hiding from the world, he had made phone calls, finding a highly regarded surgeon that was covered by our insurance and had an appointment already made for me for the following Tuesday.

Part of me wanted to leave right then, sleep in the hospital parking lot until my appointment, beg them to get me in in the three hours it would take me to get there. The other part of me wanted to go to bed, to pull the covers over my head, put on my head phones to drown out the noise. Except this noise was louder than anything I had ever heard. This noise was insufferable, inescapable. This noise could not be muffled, refused to be stifled. There WAS nowhere to hide.

We left on Monday, spending the night in the hotel connected to the hospital since my appointment was so early the next morning. We passed the time having dinner with friends that were in town as well, and my friend, Jennifer accompanied us to our room for a visit and enjoyed the laughter that always ensues when she is around.

The appointment the next morning went smoothly. I

was glad to be there, glad to get it all in motion, relieved to be doing something, anything.

My doctor had scheduled an MRI for me, to give them more information on the lump itself. The MRI was awkward but painless. I rested face down on a table. My chest lay in a cut out section. Twenty minutes that I had to remain still was bearable but the need to move wreaked havoc with my insides. What if the IV they had in my arm caused me to need to take a pee break? Could we stop and start again where we left off or would we have to start all over? What if I fell asleep and jerked like Kelley tells me I do every night? What if their idea of twenty minutes wasn't like mine? Three hours seemed pretty far from home. Did time pass differently there? I already felt like my whole world had transported to an alternate universe. Why would this be any different?

But twenty minutes was truly twenty minutes and the MRI was checked off my to-do list.

Now we just needed to chat with Dr. Margenthaler again and finalize the plan. Surgery, of course. Chemotherapy? Radiation? How much?

Instead, the meeting consisted of her telling us the MRI had revealed yet another lump in the opposite breast and she wanted an ultrasound done and another biopsy scheduled.

I tried to be tough. I tried to take it in stride. I smiled until Dr. Margenthaler left the room to send in the nurse that would lead me to get the ultrasound. The door closed and I looked into Kelley's eyes and said, "I can't do this. It's too much," and the tears began to fall.

"It's gonna be OK, baby," he said, leaning close to hold my hand, abandoning his own feelings of panic to be the stronghold I needed.

The nurse ducked her head into the room, pausing when she saw me mid-breakdown.

"Rebecca, you can come this way," she said sweetly.

"I'm sorry," I said pointing to the tears raining down my face. "I'm being a cry baby about this."

"Well, I don't blame you," she told me. "I'd be the same way."

I tried to pay attention during the ultrasound, to see anything that might look familiar from the last ultrasound I had had done. But of course, my untrained eye told me nothing.

Now all that was left to do was wait.

The biopsy couldn't be scheduled until the next morning so instead of heading home, we were in for another night in the city.

In need of a change of scenery, looking to find a place to step out of the chaos we seemed to be knee-deep in, we decided to get away for a bit and headed to the mall. I needed a minute alone. We both did, to take it in, to adjust to the new possibilities we were now faced with.

As we entered the mall, I, of course, wanted to do the obligatory bathroom visit so no shopping would be interrupted by a potty break. I left Kelley standing in the mall as I wandered down a hallway dotted with vending machines to the women's restroom, my first moments alone after hearing the chance that not just one breast was diseased, but both. My mind raced with glimpses of what my future would be like as I entered the stall, did my job and straightened my shirt tail. It was time for a stroll through the mall. Retail therapy would surely clear my mind. My hand went to the latch on the stall door and...

...nothing.

I rattled it. I shook it. I man-handled it. I used a gentle approach and softly tried to move it. And it didn't budge.

I had cancer.

Now possibly in both breasts.

And I was trapped in a bathroom stall at the Mills Mall.

I stood back from the door and, defeated, let my head flop back on my shoulders as I tilted my face to the ceiling with my eyes closed and said out loud to the vacant restroom walls, "Are you kidding me?"

And then I laughed. I laughed a big belly laugh until the tears of a shattered spirit were replaced with tears of a giggly girl.

Ok, what were my options? Any other time there would be a gaggle full of women sharing the room with me. But I was alone. And maybe that wasn't so bad after all. There was no one there to ask for help but that also meant there was no one there to see me belly crawl out from under the door. But that would be my last resort.

I could holler for Kelley but he was in the mall itself, elevator music and the shuffling of feet, conversations and squeals of children's delight surely would drown out my cries. And besides, my voice would have to carry out of the big restroom, down the hall and into the mall itself for him to hear me. That wasn't going to work.

I could wait until he decided I had been in there way too long and came to check on me. Wait! My phone. I could call him. Oh, wasn't he going to get a kick out of that?

"Hello."

"Um, Kel? Yeah, I'm trapped in the bathroom stall."

"You're WHAT? HAAAAAAAA!"

No. Maybe THAT would be my last resort.

Instead, I started digging in my purse for a makeshift tool to release me from my bonds. The weapon I chose to wield...a credit card. It's the MALL! A credit card is ANY woman's weapon at the MALL!

The latch gave in after only a small fight, the corner of the credit card sliding in just enough to free me from my jail cell.

I washed my hands and dried them, checked my hair and makeup and headed back out to find Kelley and buy myself something pretty. After all this, I definitely deserved it.

Obladi oblada.

Just like that...life goes on.

This was one of the first of many times throughout this

journey that I was taught this lesson, snapped out of a funk in a moment with an "Ohhhhhh! I get it!" See, God DOES have a sense of humor.

An ordinary girl like me goes MacGyver and is capable of escaping a bathroom stall with only the contents of her purse.

I gained a little perspective at that moment. Odd to liken breast cancer to an escape from a bathroom stall, but it was still an *A-HA* moment.

Already I would undergo surgery and treatment for breast cancer. What a blessing that in the beginning of the battle, before the swords were drawn, the truth of what I was fighting against would be completely visible.

Cancer, you can't hide from me. If you're there, I will find you and, in Jesus name, you WILL be removed from this body.

The next morning, after my second biopsy and the placement of yet another titanium marker to mark the spot, the word *benign* left the lips of my wonderful surgeon. The joy of the word and its meaning, not only for my left breast but for the battle that was to come, left us steady and ready to resume what we had come to do.

Obladi oblada.

Life goes on. And one breast or two, so does the fight.

Chapter 27

Trick elevators and shrimp on silver platters...

I worked as much as I could up until the time of my surgery, but there wasn't much time after my appointment with Dr. Margenthaler. Surgery was scheduled for a little over a week or two later. I used the time to explain to my clients what was going on and to ease my own mind knowing I had taken care of their nails until the last possible moment and made as much money as I could before I would be unable to work for an unknown amount of time.

Nearing my surgery date, one of my clients, Tisha, disappeared down the hallway to make a private phone call after I had finished with her nails and before she set off on the rest of her day.

"Becky, could you come here for a minute?" she asked beckoning me to the hallway's end.

"Sure," I said and went to her side, fearing she had received some bad news or needed my help.

"This is your confirmation number," she said handing me a slip of paper. "I think you'll be more comfortable here."

After hearing the plan I had made to stay at the hotel connected to the hospital for the nights before and after surgery, she had chosen hotel rooms for us at a hotel she was familiar with close to the hospital. I shed tears of gratitude unable to comprehend the generosity someone I knew only from our visits in my salon would show me, trying to ensure I was comfortable during this huge event in my life.

The first day of August arrived and it was time for us to head to St. Louis to prepare for my big day. Our plan was to stay in St. Louis the night before and the night after surgery; one night to prepare mentally and to give us the convenience of being near the hospital for my early morning appointment and one night to recover from any drug-induced state I might be in after surgery.

We are country people. Fancy people we are not. So when we pulled up to the front of the hotel Tisha had chosen for us, our eyes widened as a "bell boy" met us at our vehicle and promptly put our things on a luggage cart. When I go to the grocery store I generally feel guilty letting the carry out boy, who gets paid to do this very thing, tote my groceries to my car. Having someone take my luggage when Kelley, Ryan and I were completely capable seemed ridiculous.

Once inside, I gave the woman behind the counter my name and she began tip tapping away at her computer. We stood quietly, eyeing the parts of the hotel we could see from our position, already a bit intimidated by the grandness of it all, feeling so terribly guilty that this sweet friend of mine had done this for us.

"Ok, Mrs. Dennington, I have two rooms reserved for you for two nights. What credit card will you be using?" she asked.

"Uhhhhhh...credit card..." I stuttered and glanced at Kelley. I knew that hotels asked for a card sometimes to hold a room but the rooms had been reserved. If she was asking for a card at this point that could only mean she was going to charge the rooms to it. And then as I flashed back to that conversation with Tisha in the hallway and I replayed it all in my head, it hit me.

Tisha had never said she was paying for it. She had just said she thought we would be more comfortable there. Oh no!!!! I had made a HORRIBLE assumption that our already strapped finances couldn't possibly bear! And the bell boy had our luggage!

As my brain still spun, reenacting the events that brought us to this very moment, my hand steadily reached for my credit card, slowly handing it to the woman as I summoned the courage to begin the downward spiral of the next few moments.

"So what's the total on these rooms?" I asked nonchalantly as I reluctantly released my card into her hand. I think I momentarily blacked out when she told me the cost, and I knew when I came to that I had to take action and stop this fast moving train that was steadily loosening its grip on the rails.

What was I to do? Save face and just pay for it? Take the bull by the horns and just inquire if the mistake was theirs or mine? And what would Tisha think when she found out that we didn't stay at the place she had reserved for us because we couldn't afford it? Oh what a mess and we were STILL STANDING THERE!!!!!

"Ok," I said apologetically, "I was under the impression that these rooms were a gift from my friend who made the reservation."

"Well, let me see. No, it's not showing a credit card on file or that the rooms have been paid for."

"Oh, that's fine. I must have just misunderstood. You know what? Let me just shoot her a text and see what she says." I got out my phone blindly typing, trying to appear completely confident and unfazed.

Now what? What text am I supposed to send? It was already embarrassing enough that we were standing there confused with everyone watching because I had made a complete blunder and misread a generous act of a friend. The idea of the room and of her thinking of my best interest was lovely! I should never have expected her to pay for it!

My only option...fib.

I approached the desk again and told the woman that we had driven a long way and were going to leave and grab some lunch while we waited to hear from my friend and that we would be back. When actually I was climbing back in my car to head to the hotel at the hospital and pray they had rooms available.

That would have made for a smooth exit except for that dadgum bell boy who had a death grip on our luggage.

I stepped toward him and explained.

"We are going to leave and have some lunch while we wait to hear from my friend and clear up a misunderstanding about the room," I began.

"All right, ma'am, I'll take your things to your room."

You're blowing this for me bell boy!!!!! I thought.

"You know what, we'll just go ahead and take our stuff with us."

"You'll take your things with you?" he asked, confused.

I was on the edge and if he didn't hand over my stuff soon there were going to be waterworks. I was losing my hold on control.

"Yes, we'll just go ahead and take our stuff with us for now. Thank you."

Heads held high, muttering to one another under our breath "go...go...go..." the three of us hurried to the truck under the watchful and confused eyes of the valets outside, climbed in and sped away.

As I tried to explain to Kelley what had happened and where I had misunderstood, Tisha replied to my text as we pulled into the hospital/hotel parking garage.

Is there anything special I need to tell them at the desk when we check in? I had asked her, hoping this simple question would reveal where I had gone wrong.

No, she replied. *Just your name.*

Ok, thank you so much for thinking of us. It's a beautiful place but just out of our budget for right now! But I can't wait to come back some day! I typed, trying not to offend her when she had been so kind.

And my phone rang.

"Those rooms are PAID FOR!" she exclaimed, as I said hello. "Where are you?"

"We're pulling into the hospital garage!"

"Go back!" she said excitedly. "I have them on the other phone. I'll get it straightened out!"

And so we did. This time though, I had Kelley and Ryan stay in the car as I went inside to check in and then we raced to the parking garage before bell boy could get our luggage.

Luckily, the parking garage had a side elevator that we were sure would take us straight to the floors with rooms, hoping to just duck inconspicuously out of the sight of the people that had seen us in the midst of our confusion. Instead we ended up at the other end of the ground floor, the lobby still in our sights. We hurried to the elevator and stepped in, all breathing a sigh of relief as the doors closed.

Kelley pushed the button of the floor number we were headed to and we braced for the whoosh of gravity that ensues in a traveling elevator.

Nothing.

We eyed each other and waited.

Good grief we were trapped. The elevator didn't move and a hysterical giggle bubbled in my throat.

He pushed the button that would open the doors and they slid to the sides. He closed them again and pushed the number once more.

Nothing.

"Good gravy," I said, as we laughed and shook our heads. We piled out, clamoring noisily with our bags in hand and walked a few feet to a young man standing at his post that I realized was the door leading into the hotel's movie theater. I bit the bullet and approached him, surely looking a bit haggard and maybe a bit insane by now.

"Excuse me," I said. "Can you tell us how to work the elevator? We can't seem to crack the code."

I'm sure the marquis sign outside the theater was no match for the one on my forehead that flashed REDNECK over and over and over.

"There's another elevator you could try just down this way," he said pointing. "It should take your room key card with no problem."

What a graceful way he chose to set us straight and he never even rolled his eyes. Not when we were standing there at least.

Mentally smacking my forehead I said, "We'll just give this one another whirl. Thank you." And we barreled back in to the elevator we had just left, inserting our room key in the slot that we had missed before and pushed the button to our floor, shaking our heads as the elevator immediately took off.

As we opened the door to our room, I wouldn't have been surprised if angels had begun to sing. The luxury of the suite was a sight to behold. It looked as if we had stepped into a page from a magazine, the room decorated so beautifully.

My mother and stepfather set up residence in the other suite reserved for the night and soon we met up to relax for the evening. Mom and I took a long walk down the street, strolling by the numerous diners and shops and coffee houses, finally getting to visit just with one another after the whirlwind that seemed to have swept us off of our feet. As we wove our way back to the hotel, we decided to find the boys and maybe catch a movie at the theater there at our fingertips.

Windows lined the lobby area, letting us see into the theater area itself and catch a glimpse of the concession stand and theater doors leading to the movie showing in each room. Outside each theater room that was dismissing its moviegoers stood a hotel staff member dressed in black and white holding a silver tray that each ticket holder removed a treat from.

"I think they're serving shrimp!" mom said.

"Shrimp? Where?" I asked, my nose wrinkling up.

"Outside the doors of the movies. Those people have silver trays with shrimp on them," she said.

We chose to see "Dinner for Schmucks" that night. I had never heard of it and frankly could have cared less. I was starting to get a little anxious about why I was there in the first place and any distraction was much needed. The movie, to this day, is one of my favorites. I laughed so hard out loud that Kelley even asked me once if I was going to be ok.

Yeah. I sure was.

The movie ended and we got up from our seats, chattering to one another about the movie, reenacting our favorite parts. As we reached the door to exit the room, there stood a girl with a silver tray…

Covered in tootsie rolls and peppermints, not shrimp.

"Oh," was all mom said when I turned and nodded toward the tray.

The surgery was definitely a monumental event in my life, the idea that its whole purpose was to rid my body of cancer was definitely sobering. But I don't remember it. How could I? I was asleep. But more importantly, WHY should I? I was surrounded by family and friends. My husband and son, my parents, my friends, Jennifer, Robin, Mike, Jared and Susan. We stood together in the waiting room in a circle as we prayed together before I left with the nurse. I laid in a hospital bed in purple socks supplied by the hospital after they started my IV, as each of the people there waiting with me that day took their turn to hug me before they took me back. I was nestled in the arms of ones who loved me, carried through the surgery by the prayers of these people and countless others whose spirits held my hand.

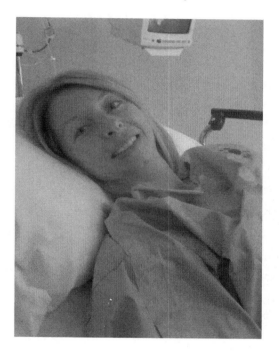

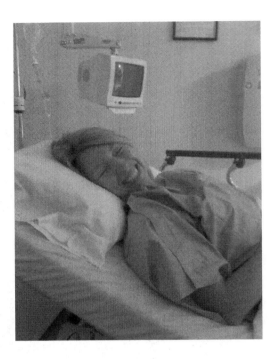

Memories of the surgery are, of course, non-existent. I have a foggy memory of the operating room, sliding from one table to another. My next memory, a vague recollection of the recovery room I was in, the nurse explaining that I could do no tugging or pulling or lifting and Kelley saying, "So does that mean she can't mow tomorrow?" and the nurse taking him seriously and saying "Oh, no." I remember looking into my son's eyes as I groggily pointed his direction and said "I love him." I remember the comfort of seeing my father by my side as I began to come around.

There is little I remember except for these few things.

When I think of my surgery, a smile slides across my face and a chuckle escapes my lips. I remember no traumatizing recovery. The brief nausea I encountered after being sedated is a dull memory.

What I remember of the time I had surgery is the hands of people who love me squeezing my own. What I remember about the time I had surgery is the lovely dinner we had at such a luxurious hotel that we stayed in because of the sweet heart of a beautiful friend. What I remember about the time I had surgery was being outsmarted by an elevator and worrying if it was going to seem rude when I didn't eat any of that shrimp they were serving off of that silver platter.

I remember laughing.

And that's fine by me.

"Dad always thought laughter was the best medicine, which I guess is why several of us died of tuberculosis."

--Jack Handey, "Deep Thoughts," *Saturday Night Live*

Chapter 28

Wish you were here...

Now that I have delved into the emotional deep and told the stories of some memorable occasions to say the least, the beginning of my chest-baring experiences, I am led now back to more current events.

Back to radiation.

I believe it was the day of my last chemo that I rang the bell and then set off downstairs to begin the next leg of my journey.

They called it a simulation. I couldn't tell you why. I called it my mapping because the purpose of the appointment was to mark off the area that they would be doing the radiation treatment on. This appointment was more than an examination that lasted 30 uncomfortable seconds. This appointment consisted of me on a table, naked from the waist up, with two or three women drawing on me with a paint pen. I can't be too detailed about this particular experience because, having just left chemotherapy, I was out of it from the Benadryl and the memories are vague.

I do remember that once I arrived in the room and gowned up, (open in the front), and they settled me on the table, a blood test that they had to have done (as a technicality) to ensure I wasn't pregnant before starting this process was held up in the lab. I'm already a pretty patient person so I wasn't all messed up about the wait and plus I was so tired from the meds I had just received (and probably from the relief of knowing that five months of chemo was finally finished), I would have been more than happy to simply doze on the table until they were ready to begin.

Except that the table I was laying on for some reason made me think of a diving board. There was no cushion or padding. Just a narrow table. I remember laying there, so tired, my whole body undoubtedly touching the table but still feeling as if I was going to fall off at any moment. And every time I dozed off, I jerked awake having just imagined my arm had slipped off the table and would surely drag my body with it. Like that video you see of a sleeping cat falling off of a windowsill or into an aquarium. I'm sure the cat wasn't embarrassed at all. But I was going to be.

Eventually they were able to complete what needed to be done. They measured and marked, drew and calculated and then they used small clear pieces of tape to cover parts of the markings to increase the chances that what they had just worked so hard on wouldn't completely wash off in the three weeks' time that would pass before I would be back to begin the actual radiation.

And then there were the tattoos.

I assume as "back-up" after they placed markings, lines and circles in red and blue on, above and below my breast, and because it was important that these markings stay put or were fairly easily reproduced, they used something like an ink filled needle to place blue dots on certain points throughout this treasure map on my chest. Seven blue dots that will never go away.

My friend, Summer, suggested I ask them to put the dots in a pattern. I thought this was a great idea. But when I asked them if they could put the tattoos in a design like a constellation or something so that we could connect them and come out with the Big Dipper or something like that, they politely said no and gave me the look. Tough crowd.

I flip flop between "Oh well, what's a few more markings on my chest!" to "Now, dang it. Isn't my body scarred up enough already? If I'd wanted a tattoo, I would have gotten one by now! And now I get 7 STUPID BLUE

DOTS!"

Since the beginning, I have kept things from this journey. Mementos of where I've been, reminders of a certain moment, good or bad, that I wanted to earmark in time. I have every card I received in a little box under my bed. I have hospital bracelets and hotel room key cards (was I not supposed to keep those?). I have photos and emails and texts saved so that I never forget.

How is it that I think I ever could?

Like a weary traveler and a travel-worn suitcase covered in luggage labels, each sticker like a check mark revealing where I've been, a collection of post cards to show the path I have been on, I hold my souvenirs from this trip close to my chest.

The tiny scar on my breast from the biopsy, marking the moment my life changed forever.

The scar from my lumpectomy, marking the beginning of the battle.

The scar from the port they placed in my chest, marking a direct route for the chemotherapy like a sheath to a sword.

And now, seven blue tattoos, tiny dots marking the final stages of war we rage against this enemy that has threatened to steal my life and break my spirit.

Far from home, far from my family, I have now gathered the final of my souvenirs from this journey and continue the last leg of the battle that brings me home to you.

Wish you were here…

Chapter 29

Am I radiant yet?...

My ability to chatterbox my way through all uncomfortable procedures and appointments throughout this ordeal eluded me in the first few days of radiation. I suppose it was different for many reasons. Other appointments where I sat for an examination were quick for the most part. I sat on the table and the nurse or doctor would ask me to open my gown and after a quick once-over, I was allowed to cover back up. Radiation on your breast isn't quite like that.

Every day I hop off the shuttle and make my way to the elevator with my Hope Lodge friends who have appointments close to the same time as mine. I walk into the radiation department through the sliding doors, say hello to Dot and Hope at the desk, scan the barcode on the back of my card that alerts them in the back that I am there for my appointment and head back to gown up and wait in a room designated for women getting radiation for breast cancer. It is a comfort most days to see familiar faces there, other women going through what I am, just at different stages. I met Beverly, a feisty little lady who, after a mastectomy, was receiving radiation. I sat every day with her as we waited for our names to be called, I enjoyed her company and the stories she told of her life. I was grateful to have crossed paths with her and her sweet daughter, Karen, and rejoiced with them when her radiation was complete and her life would go on outside those doors while my own journey would continue on.

They call my name and I follow a tech to the radiation area. At this point each day, they make the same request and I oblige.

"Name?"

"Rebecca Dennington"

"And what are we doing radiation on?"

"My right breast."

The repetition of it and my need to make things flow smoothly brings me to answer without being asked anymore. "Rebecca Dennington, right breast," I now say when we arrive at the computer. Such a habit that now no matter what doctor I'm seeing, I have to fight the urge to say these words automatically, which makes for an uncomfortable moment when they have simply asked for my birth date.

The first few radiations were uncomfortable for me. Each day my radiation was done by basically the same people. Some days there were maybe five or six techs in the room, other days four, three, still some days only two. The mix of technicians was always of the same group for me, and I'm just going to be honest and say, no matter how vain it may sound, it would have just been a lot easier if they had been ugly people. But no. Each day I lay on a table, my chest exposed, arms above my head in stirrups, surrounded by a group of attractive people that could have been faces on *Grey's Anatomy*. So here I am, mostly bald, overweight, trying to nonchalantly pull my pants up over my fat roll just in case they catch a glimpse while getting me settled on the table. I fight the urge every day to say, "You know I haven't always looked like this." I'm sure, though, that they could have cared less.

In the beginning, it took a little bit longer to get the kinks worked out, to get me set up just right, follow my markings and my tattoos to position me just so so that the same area got the radiation every day.

"Just lay heavy," they would tell me.

That's not as easy as it sounds. I wanted to help. If I saw they were trying to move me to the left a little, well, I wanted to move left. But that was going to have moved me too far. So even now, I just have to concentrate on relaxing and being still, letting them maneuver my body wherever they need. So many times now, as I lay there one of them has gently pushed my side, moving me only a fraction to get me in just the right spot. And each time, I inwardly cringe imagining what it must look like for them to be pressing on my untoned flesh. Visions of the Pillsbury Doughboy commercial where the hand pokes him in his soft belly play in my head and make me want to giggle each time. And then the first few times they had to slide me down the table by the sheet I was laying on or shake the table to move me that miniscule little bit to get me just right, causing my body to surely jiggle like a Jell-O mold, made me grateful that my head has to be turned away from them for the procedure so I don't see the look on their faces when they see the ripple effect happening on my gut. The first few radiations were hard. They weren't painful. But being laid out, my bare breast being manipulated by strangers, made me embarrassed deep down inside and it was a hard pill to swallow. With my head turned, I would find anything to stare at, the clock, the wall, the shelving, feigning deep interest in anything I could light my eyes on. At a certain point they engage the machinery above me and it slowly slides over to my left, and each and every time, one of the technicians appears out of nowhere, either popping up behind the machine or leaning quickly over the table to put their hand between the machine and my elbow at the last second, protecting me from harm. They always have CDs playing in the background and I would focus on the music until they said, "Ok, we're going to get you going," and they left me alone in the room to receive the treatment.

Once they leave the room, the machine engages and I hear a hum as the radiation beam is activated. From the left I watch the computer screen hanging from the wall counting up to 25 and the humming stops. The machine slides over me to the other side and then I count down with the hum for another 30 seconds, praying I don't sneeze, rolling my eyes in irritation at myself if I forget and sigh, hoping I haven't heaved too big of a breath that I might have moved myself out of alignment.

Vulnerable, exposed, embarrassed…those are all the things I feel every day.

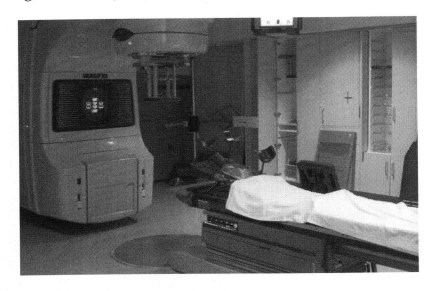

But time and the experience have been kind to me and as the new has worn off, my comfort zone has expanded and I am much more at ease these days. These people have become my friends, these technicians who each day wallow my body into position to perform this radiation, this treatment I look at like an act of "sealing the deal," singeing the edges of a rope so it doesn't fray again. Their cheerful faces greet me each day. They never miss a beat as they watch me take off my head scarf that I have given up now during my treatment, smile at me when I jokingly ask if my hair is messed up. The procedure now so run of the mill that my motor mouth runs again at full speed as they ask me about my day, about what I did on the weekend or my upcoming plans with Kelley and the kids. I pause long enough for them to leave the room and the beams of light to shine on my breast to keep the cancer at bay, and then the conversation picks up where we left off as they reenter my vision and help me up off the table, off to wait for Juanita to pick us up in the shuttle and return us to our home to pass the time until we turn in, resting up for another day.

Each morning I have my prescribed regimen of corn starch to help prevent my clothes from rubbing and each night a coating of a prescription cortisone cream and a layer of Vanicream. I'm so greasy I'm surprised I don't slide out of bed at night.

As of right now, my skin is pink and slightly uncomfortable like the worst sunburn ever but is in better condition at this point than they expected. I certainly won't complain though. Every meal I sit in the dining room and eat whatever strikes my fancy. While my friends receiving treatment on their faces or throats fight the blisters in their mouths and miss the taste of food.

I miss home terribly and yet look for the bright spots in every day. That is my choice.

I am warm. I am safe. I am fed. I am where I am supposed to be.

I am just not where I belong.

Chapter 30

Just call me Carl...

Sarah Beth is four. Except, now, after being informed by her that she's "really getting tired of her middle name", I only call her Sarah. She runs and she plays. She hides behind columns in the dining room and jumps out and hollers, "HEY!" She sits on my lap sometimes and plays the "Talking Tom" game on my iPhone, a game where a cat named Tom purrs when you rub his belly, yells "YOW!" when you touch his tail, falls down if you tap him too many times and repeats everything you say. "Hi Tom!" "Hel-LO Tom!" "I love you!" she says to him, waiting for him to repeat it. Once after she was a little bored with Tom, we went shopping in the App. Store on the phone to find a new talking friend. There was one called Talking Carl that we tried to get but there was a problem and it didn't go through. Just a little while later, she ran back up to me and I asked if she remembered my name.

"Yes!" she said.

"What is it?" I asked her.

"Carl!"

She's a four-year-old, never ending bundle of energy. Until this week. The radiation she receives is beginning to make her tired. She slept, breathing loudly upside down on the couch in the dining area a couple of days ago, and it gave me a chance to have some mommy talk with Sarah's mother, Mary.

Sarah has Retinoblastoma, a rare form of cancer in the retina of her eye. Diagnosed at the age of 8 months, she has already lost sight on her left side and has a glass eye. The cancer though has moved to the other eye and now she stays at Hope Lodge with her mother while she gets radiation to save the sight that she has left. The radiation is not only an attempt to stop the cancer from robbing her of her vision completely, but also is an attempt to stop it from spreading to the eye socket and then on to her brain.

"Then we'll lose her. I can deal with her not being able to see. But I can't imagine not having HER," Mary said to me.

The conversation ended soon after; Mary went on to visit with the others in the dining room. I, however, had to escape to my room because of the lump in my throat.

I lay on a table every day, uncomfortable because my breasts are exposed to everyone in the room, and wait for them to shoot me with radioactive beams. My skin is turning pink. I am beginning to feel heat on the inside of the area they are treating. Fatigue is setting in.

But Mary goes every day and waits anxiously in the waiting room, while they put sweet Sarah to sleep so she won't move while they do radiation on her eye.

I am away from my husband and my children and I cry when they leave me on the weekends.

Mary is away from her husband and children, while she is here fighting to save her daughter's life, doing everything that she can to ensure that Sarah doesn't just get to see her family next weekend, but that she gets to see them when she is five, and 10, and on her graduation day and her wedding day and when she has babies of her own.

Kelley and I try to think of fun things to do with the kids the next time they come up to see me, to make the most of our time together, to make up for me being gone.

If radiation doesn't work like they hope, Mary is having to try and think of all the things she wants Sarah to see before she loses the sight in her other eye and darkness falls over her.

I have scars on my chest now…

But I can see.

My breast is smaller now due to surgery and treatment.

But I am alive.

I am far from home.

But my children are fine.

"Hey! I remember you!" Sarah says excitedly now every time she sees me.

Yes, Sarah, and I will ALWAYS remember you. Thank you for the lesson.

Chapter 31

My best friend, Bob...

When I was 13 or so, I went to a summer camp called RTI. Kids from all different schools in the area were chosen to attend a week-long camp where we talked about peer pressure and learned the bad effects of drugs. We were split into small groups that met throughout the day. If I remember correctly, it was a time set aside on the schedule where the kids assigned to that specific group got to have deep talks, almost like a mini therapy session. By the end of the week, the bond formed with the others in the small group allowed us to feel free to reveal our innermost secrets or hurts or questions. Needless to say, we formed very special bonds with the other kids that on the first day were strangers and by the end, our newest close friends. We made warm fuzzies, yarn necklaces that we passed on to other campers like a little fuzzy hug. The other students from my school that I went to the camp with were already some of my best friends, this experience bonding us tighter, expanding our little circle with the new friends we made.

Hope Lodge is almost like my new summer camp. Except that I have shown up by myself. It is not summer. I am not 13.

The first few days I went to the dining area to eat a meal or get a snack or drink a soda, I took my trusty iPad with me and my earphones and sat alone while I watched *Eat, Pray, Love* or *Burlesque* over and over. Now I sit and enjoy my snack or meal with my new friends, visiting while our sweet Sarah watches Scooby Doo on my iPhone. Her momma, quick with a solution like mommies have to be sometimes, places a dishtowel on her head to keep my earphones from slipping off of her little ears. We visit and giggle. When she giggles, Sarah, is unaware in her innocence of the special place in our hearts we all have for her in just the little time we have known her.

I knew that when I came up here I would meet some new people, make a new friend or two. But I mainly pictured myself alone, maybe volunteering at the chemo treatment area at the hospital because that's where I've spent the last four or five months and that's where I would feel most comfortable. Or maybe volunteering to go grab lunch for Dr. Pluard and his nurse Michelle, who put up with so many calls from Kelley and I during my treatments.

I expected to spend my days alone. I never expected my comfort zone to be right here at Hope Lodge.

Kelley stayed with me the first three days of treatment. He drove me the first day. We rode the shuttle the second day. The third day I drove, wanting my first time driving there and parking in the parking garage to be with Kelley's supervision. My first day on my own I rode the shuttle again. I was still unsure of the schedule but being a country girl that lives on gravel and where there is gravel, there isn't much traffic, I was a bit nervous about driving myself the few blocks between me and Barnes-Jewish. Ok, so here's the thing. Directions just aren't my thing. Kelley just drives and seems to get me where I need to be while I am snoozing or gabbing or texting or digging in my purse, oblivious to what road we are on or which way we turned or what lane to be in. Times that I HAVE chimed in to help with directions, I have contributed to the confusion of the moment, making the level of marital stress in the vehicle reach the danger zone and have often been instructed by Kelley with the words,"Ok, Magellan, don't try to help."

On Tuesdays, I do, however, drive myself to the hospital for treatment because I also see the doctor that day and the last Tuesday I tried utilizing the shuttle, it got me there with time to spare, but when my appointment ran late, I missed my return trip to the Lodge. Deciding I wasn't interested in waiting two hours for the next shuttle ride, I walked back. In my head scarf and Kelley's coat, nose running like a faucet because of the cool air, I was a sight to behold. And although no one in their right mind would have wanted to kidnap ME, my hand was on my mace.

All the other days though, the convenience of the shuttle won out and I board the shuttle and wander to a seat close to the back. Others from the Lodge climb on as well and we are off on our pick up route to the hospital. From Hope Lodge our next stop is the Ronald McDonald House where we pick up the mothers and families of babies that are being cared for at Children's Hospital. Then on to Barnes Lodge, a place that offers the families of patients rooms for $30.00 a night that is in close proximity to the hospital.

Each day is a 15-20 minute ride for us Hope Lodgers, a few minutes that can seem like a lifetime in silence. So each day we climb on the shuttle in our imaginary assigned seats and small talk our way to treatment. And then when our treatments are finished, once we all got our routines established, we eventually began meeting back up in the lobby to wait for Juanita, the shuttle driver to return, the bonds of our newly formed family life drawing us toward one another as we made the unspoken choice to gather together rather than separate and wait alone.

Other than our little Sarah, I believe I am the youngest of the crew here for an extended stay. But as cancer is no respecter of persons, neither is friendship.

It was on my initial solo shuttle rides that I began my small talk conversations with Bob. His chosen habitual seat mirrored mine in the back of the shuttle, and each day we visited across the aisle as our white carriage barreled down the streets of St. Louis. I remember our first conversation being about his home in Glen Allen, a town not nearly an hour from my own, only minutes from my nephew. He spoke of the history of the town, stories that I repeated to Kelley as I stood that day in the cold waiting for the shuttle to come back and pick me up. This was before I was familiar with the time schedule and was afraid to venture too far from the shuttle's arrival spot in fear of missing my ride. It was a super cold day and as I spoke to Kelley on the phone, shivering and watching my breath, I remember seeing a hooded man in my peripheral vision standing behind me but disappearing after a few minutes. Later the hooded man caught my eye again and I realized it was Bob.

"I saw you standing out here and I thought maybe you knew something I didn't know about the shuttle so I came out too. Then I just decided you were crazy," he said.

Our conversations continued on our daily rides to and from treatment. He had been in the service and so had my father. In fact, when my father came to visit, they spoke for a while and knew many of the same people.

Bob loves to fish and so does Kelley. I would never make a good fisherman because the only lures I would buy would be the pretty ones. Plus fish smell bad and there are no potties on a bass boat. So as for personal fishing experiences to share, I had none. But I had a few of Kelley's in my back pocket to tell.

Daily shuttle rides extended to conversations on the park bench outside the Lodge as we awaited our pick-up. When I called home my stories were all Bob stories. In time when I spoke of him I always began with, "You know, my best friend, Bob,"

The cancer Bob was receiving treatment for is squamous cell carcinoma. His cancer in his nose. Every day I go and lay down on a table, told to lay heavy, passed twice with radiation beams. Every day Bob lies down on the table and they put a form over his entire face and bolt it to the table. Restraints connected by elastic bungee cords are placed on his ankles and wrists so that when he straightens out his legs it pulls his arms and shoulders down as well to keep them out of the way. My chest feels sun burned. His face is red and painful, his top lip sometimes swollen. As the days progress, I watch him trying to eat mashed potatoes and see the pain and frustration in his face. And yet he continues to fight.

It is better to be in chains with friends, than in a garden with strangers. –Persian Proverb

Radiation and chemotherapy are the chains of cancer. And I suppose here at Hope Lodge, we are bonded by our chains. Here I have a new family of survivors. I spend my days with people I can relate to because of the cancer we have in common, because of the chains that, for now, hold us down. But only for now. Those chains will be removed, this bondage broken.

Until then, we continue to fight, me and my best friend, Bob.

Chapter 32

Just us in a sock...

It was a down day.

I wasn't in the pits of despair. I never got that down.
Just tired.

Until the age of 35, I had spent my life being stubborn
about the flu or a cough. I self-diagnosed my own kidney
stones, able to recognize the small sticker burr-looking rock I
passed because of my best friend, Google.

I could probably count doctor appointments on one
hand that weren't yearly Pap smears. It seemed each time I
caved and went to the doctor, either I felt better by the time
the appointment rolled around or I convinced myself that if I
had just waited another day, my body would have healed on
its own and that I had just frivolously spent money I hadn't
needed to spend. If I would have just been tougher...

Now here I am, hanging out at a medical facility every
single day. In the last year, I have been poked and prodded
and examined almost constantly it seems and it can definitely
wear a person down.

What I do every day is really no big deal. I'm not out
of breath after radiation. I don't cry because of pain too tough
to bear.

This day I simply cried because I was tired of the whole
mess, in the middle of an emotional decline I knew was only
temporary. It had happened before and I had made it to the
other side and I knew I would again.

For right then though, I was in the middle of a pity
party and the people I most wanted to invite were 300 miles

away.

I remember telling Kelley on the phone that day that I was mopey. I was tired. I was lonely and I hadn't slept in my own bed in almost two weeks.

The next day I was going to be going to my first doctor appointment alone which was no big deal but still a first for me. Kelley and the kids weren't going to be able to come up until Saturday afternoon and I suppose the idea of all the extra alone time on my hands was weighing on me.

"Why don't I just come home tomorrow? I could leave right after my radiation and surprise the kids," I said.

"Babe, I just don't feel comfortable with you driving home alone, especially with that belt about to go out on your truck," he said apologetically.

"I'll be fine," I insisted.

"No. We'll just come to you. I'll get the kids up Saturday morning and we'll head out. We'll be there by 11:30 at the latest. Look, I'm about to pull up to your mom's and pick up the kids. Why don't you get some rest and me and the kids will call you about 5:30."

Hanging up I felt even mopier.

You're not the boss of me, I thought to myself. *He can't tell me I can't drive home. I'm a GROWN UP!* And no, I had never driven that far by myself and ESPECIALLY in city traffic, but I was pretty sure I could do it. The ride back on Sunday would be horribly lonely but I could cry all the way if I wanted!

Just thinking about the whole mess made me tired and so by 5:00 I was in my pink fuzzy jammy pants, mismatched tank top, furry and partially shiny bald head free of its usual covering.

I lay in bed fighting with the scratched *Friends* DVD I was watching, wondering if bedtime would EVER get here.

And then there was a knock at the door.

No one ever knocks on my door. Were they getting together downstairs for Bingo? Maybe it was one of the other

Lodgers just hoping to visit or maybe one of them was sick.

I jumped off of the bed and scrambled to get my head scarf back on and adjusted. I leaned against the door and pressed my eye to the peephole.

No one.

I had taken too long to get my head covered and I had missed my only visitor to my room ever.

I stepped back and turned the door handle, opening the door to reveal the empty hallway. I moved my foot to step out and then magically...

Kelley stood before me.

"WHAT ARE YOU DOING HERE?" I screeched, throwing my arms around him.

"I came to go with you to your doctor appointment tomorrow."

"You did?" I asked still stunned.

"And then... I'm going to take you home."

No sweeter words had ever reached my ears and as my arms tightened around him, the tears began to flow. While I had been trying to convince him to let me drive home to him, he had been covering for the fact that he was already on his way to me.

I slept in my own bed that weekend. The first glimpses of each room in my house brought a sigh to my lips, peace to my heart.

I was home.

As wonderful as the weekend was, it made it so much harder to watch them pull away from the drive at Hope Lodge, leaving me behind as they journeyed back to the home that felt so different to them with me not in it. My heart breaks every time I watch that red truck drive away, Kelley's hand signing *I Love You*, my children's hands hanging out their windows waving goodbye as I stand stubbornly on the sidewalk until they mix into the traffic and I can no longer see them.

The lonely is worse when they leave. I spend the week

adjusting to the quiet just to have to start from scratch on Sunday when they leave me again.

We were blessed that the six weeks I am gone fall where I will spend no holidays away from home.

Except for one.

St. Patrick's Day.

Our 16th wedding anniversary.

Never have we been apart on our wedding anniversary. But I would happily miss this one anniversary to ensure I will be around for the next one hundred of them...give or take a few. Falling on a Thursday made it impossible to work it out to be together so we would just celebrate a day or two late when they came up to visit for the weekend.

I was standing in my bathroom at the mirror this St. Patrick's Day when I heard a shuffle on the floor beside me. A piece of notebook paper lay folded on the floor that hadn't been there before. I assumed at first it had just fallen off my desk where I had been working minutes before but then I realized I hadn't been writing on notebook paper. I unfolded it to find the words *Happy Anniversary* beautifully written in pencil, flowers decorating the page.

I slammed my eye to the peephole and there stood Kelley.

"Happy Anniversary," he said as I opened the door.

"I can't believe you're here! Where are the kids?" I asked.

"They're right downstairs," he said.

And just like that, all was right in my world. There we were. Together again. The four of us.

Yes. It's MY cancer.

But it's been OUR battle.

My cheerleaders. My rocks. My reasons for fighting as hard as I do.

When we are together, that is when I am strongest, unbeatable.

While going through my chemo treatments, I had a phone conversation with a friend and nail client of mine, Ruby. She was telling me how proud she was of the way my husband and children stuck by me so closely and took such good care of me.

"It's like seeing all of you in a big sock," she said.

"A sock?" I asked.

"Yeah. A sock. Pantyhose style. It stretches as it needs to."

Now that's a deep thought. And I totally got it.

Kelley and the kids just pulled away for the last time. After spending the weekend together they are headed home to pass the last days without me with them.

Only moments after they left, Kelley sent me a text.

Look under your laptop. I left you something.

As if on a treasure hunt, I raced back up to my room, slowly lifting the laptop, enjoying the anticipation.

An envelope lay underneath, inside a card with a shy looking puppy on it.

Pretend that I'm with you.......it read on the front, *because, in my heart, I am.*

And then in Kelley's handwriting, *This is the last time I have to have my heart break because I am leaving you behind. In a few short days I will be bringing you home for good. Until then, know I am with you in my heart. Love, your husband.*

This journey is almost finished. No more broken hearts. Soon I will be on the road to home.

I think these pantyhose have been stretched enough.

Families are the compass that guides us. They are the inspiration to reach great heights, and our comfort when we occasionally falter.
--Brad   *Henry*

Chapter 33

Breathe...

It has almost been six weeks now since I left my home and moved into my new temporary one. Used to my little country town where life is quiet and you rarely meet a stranger, life here was sure to lie at the opposite end of the spectrum. Before Kelley left to head back home and try to get the kids' lives settled into some kind of order during my time away, he did everything he could to settle mine as well, making sure that I had everything I needed. Food, water, mace, gas in the car...I was set. I crossed the street occasionally to piddle around Walgreen's or walked to the Schnucks that sits on the block behind Hope Lodge. But as for me going anywhere, it just wasn't necessary and frankly, I was a bit chicken to drive.

At the end of my fourth weekend here, after Kelley and the kids left from our weekend visit and I was trying to readjust once more to my week-day life of solitude, the sunshine out my window caught my eye and I had to get out in it. Normally if I wanted to take a walk, I just walked out the front door and headed off down the street. That day it was officially the first day of spring. And I needed more. I grabbed my purse and keys, signed out and jumped in my car. I was headed to Forest Park.

To most people this would be no big deal. But for me this was an act of courage! I had gone for a walk there once with my friend, Jennifer and then Kelley and the kids and I had gone during one of their visits. I, however, had never driven myself anywhere up here except my short drive to and from the hospital, to Schnucks and to my doctors' appointments. Oh, and once I hit Arby's down the street. But no further. Here I was just being big and driving my little self right on over there like I knew where I was going!

I pulled into the parking lot, already so proud that I had made it there safe and sound. And then...I simply walked. So used to checking in and always telling someone where I was going to be at back home, that day I stepped out of my car, locked it up, and just walked away. I could have headed out in a million different directions...A bicycle path here, a bridge over there, a path this way. It was a sense of freedom I had never experienced. The park seemed to go on forever and I was free to enjoy as much of it as I wanted.

I had pictured myself walking, head down, earphones in my ears, counting off songs until I could say I made it through a thirty minute walk. But as the music began to play and I began plotting my route, I started noticing not just the park but what was happening all around me. It was the beginning of one of my "moments."

One of my favorite movies, *Love Actually*, starts out and ends with scenes in an airport while Hugh Grant's voice tells us about how we seem to live in a time where, more often than not, we are reminded that this world is full of anger and sadness and all things bad. But a simple look around an arrivals gate at an airport can remind you of the good parts we DON'T hear about every day. Families reuniting, a glowing newlywed couple returning from their honeymoon, a young mother and father meeting their baby daughter for the first time, a mother's hand reaching for the hand of her son who is returning from war. Stories of real life, some of the good moments, playing out right before your eyes.

As I began my walk that day, at first my mind focused only on choosing which way to go, I saw only a crowded park. People walking everywhere, some with strollers, some with dogs. Some were running or walking, dressed for the part with headphones and MP3 players, running clothes and tennis shoes.

I soon realized that I was walking at a hurried pace for no reason, heading who-knew-where fast. "Where's the fire?" I thought to myself. "What's the rush?" I guess that's kind of been my mindset though for these last eight or so months. Racing toward the end of this cancer mess. So ready to be done with treatments, to get our lives back in some kind of order, to get MY life back. Maybe my feet haven't been running but my mind has been. Eye on the prize, caught up in the battle, swimming toward the surface with my lungs full of air.

Breathe.

As I steadied my pace and let my eyes wander my surroundings, Dub Pierce's voice rang through my headphones. My iPod, set to shuffle, delivering the words to his beautiful song "Adore."

"Glory be to the Almighty King,

Abba, Father, maker of me,

You are the one that I do adore

The reason I breathe and I sing for..."

As I stepped in and out of the flow of people, I noticed a young man sitting in the shade of a tree. His legs at a V out in front of him, a baby nestled there facing him, his own legs a tiny reflection of his father's. Appearing to not quite yet be mobile, the little one sat enamored with the grass. Appearing at ease as though he had nowhere to go and nowhere else he'd rather be, the young father sat enamored with his son.

Sunlight filtered through the trees as I followed the path. Picnic baskets and blankets were scattered here and there in the green grass that seemed to have magically sprouted overnight. I followed a concrete path up a paved hill, climbing steps that led to the World's Fair Pavilion. A man sat inside with a set of bongo-like drums, playing a steady beat while he let children shake what seemed to be a bumpy gourd full of beans. I paused for a minute to read the board that held the history of the pavilion itself and as I turned to walk out, I was caught off guard by the view. "On top of the world," I thought. I stood at the edge of the Pavilion, atop a grassy hill that melted into a green covered field.

I found a concrete block, part of the gorgeous landscaping weaved throughout the park, and sat in wonderment, watching the scenes of life playing out in front of me. Perched on this spot of my own, I felt compelled to take a moment and absorb the view. I had time.

Breathe.

I watched two young boys roll on their sides down the hill and hop up ready to continue tossing their football and smiled to myself when I realized I was fighting the urge to roll after them. I saw a mommy and daddy folding up their blankets and gathering their things, their little one taking still unsure first steps, flopping hard on its rump more than once and popping back up to stumble and thump again.

I stepped down from my perch and resumed my walk, intent on memorizing every scene playing out around me. A mother and son flying a kite, heads tilted together, watching it as it danced like the gentle winds' puppet. I slowed my walk to look behind me and take a backwards glance at the hill I had just descended. A lone blanket lay in the middle, two people napping, a knee up and arms draped over their faces, so their eyes were shielded from the sun but their bodies could soak up its warmth.

Down the path, more blankets littered the ground under trees and in small clearings, picnic baskets and coolers. I watched a couple tossing a Frisbee back and forth as I passed and wondered what they chatted about during their leisurely game. Four boys raced around with a football, falling in a pile and then assessing the damage when one of the four became a casualty in the game, tears shed to wash away the pain from a pile up gone wrong. The biggest boy who held the ball coaxing the wounded to return to the game.

I glanced at my watch. Unbelievably forty minutes had passed. The sun was setting but there was still time. Time for one more scene.

The Boat House Restaurant nestled at the heart of the park almost, sits on a small "lake." I walked by and watched families in paddle boats, slowly moving through the water among the ducks, neither in any hurry, the sun's golden glow reflecting off the water. A family walked along the water's edge, stopping and directing one another to stand here or there or just so by that beautiful blooming tree so they could snap a shot with their camera and remember that moment forever. Two best girl friends sat on a park bench, relaxing and enjoying good conversation.

A couple, strolling, holding hands, the man not leading but walking steady beside his wife, her head beautifully wrapped in a lovely printed chemo scarf.

The day was drawing to a close and I headed back to my car, filled with a renewed sense of peace. I walked in the sun that day until I broke through the water's surface, letting go of what I had been hanging on to so tightly for so long.

In two days, I will receive my last radiation treatment. I will say goodbye to my new family here at Hope Lodge that I've been honored to share a home with for six weeks. And I will say goodbye to the friends that performed my treatments, friendly faces that I have looked forward to seeing each day. I will walk through the door for the last time, pass Dot and Hope at the desk, this time without saying, "See ya tomorrow."

I will once again and for the final time... ring the bell.

And I will take Kelley's hand and we will walk away, leaving cancer behind.

My winter is over.

I have been reborn. Re-newed. Stripped and built back up.

My spring is here.

The battle is done.

...And I win.

The Lord will rescue me from every evil attack and will bring me safely to His heavenly kingdom. To Him be the glory forever and ever. Amen. – 2 Timothy 4:18

About the Author

Raised in Bernie, Missouri, a small mid-American farming town, where one single caution light marks the center and a traffic jam is two cars creeping behind a combine, Becky Dennington grew up a member of a tight-knit community of about 2000 people. Today, after 36 years, she still resides in her hometown. Married to her best friend for 16 years, mother to a son and a daughter, she has enjoyed working as a nail technician for the last 11 years in a little building shaped like a barn.

In July of 2010, Becky's life took a difficult turn when she was diagnosed with breast cancer. Having the heart of a writer, she found comfort in documenting her journey by starting a blog. Deep Thoughts by Beck began as a way for Becky to process her thoughts and feelings of dealing with the stress of a cancer diagnosis. She soon found it was a wonderful way to keep family and friends updated on the progress of her treatments and in time, was blessed to see that it began to encourage women she knew to be more proactive in early detection.

Becky's blog has now taken the shape of her first published work, Me and the Ugly C. Today, as well as being a breast cancer survivor, she happily adds author to her list of accomplishments.

<u>Acknowledgments:</u>

To God – For Your everlasting love, for Your patience with me, for Your forgiveness and for the blessings You pour out upon me each and every day.

To my mother, Dottie Babb, and my father, Bill Kirkwood – For loving me like you do.

To Steve Babb, Ganny (Jean Babb), Linda Bode and my Gran Gran (Donna Kirkwood) – for being part of who I am.

To Cory Blocker – for believing in me

To Staci Taylor and Mark McConnell at Lazy Day Publishing – for making my dream come true

To Dr. Jennifer Waller, Dr. Julie Margenthaler, Dr. Timothy Pluard, Dr. Imran Zoberi – for saving my life

To Jennifer Becking – for your faithful friendship and for your house key

To my family and friends in Bernie, MO and neighboring communities - for your love, prayers and generosity.

To Julie Dodd – for capturing those precious moments that I'll treasure forever and for the friendship that came from it all.

To our pastor Jared Owens and our church family at SEMO Community Church – for your comfort, love and prayers.

And last but not least…

To 18 Fore Life – I am honored to be an 18 Fore Life love offering recipient and to be associated with such an amazing charity. **www.18forelife.com**

In loving memory of my Papa, Clyde "Cotton" Babb and Uvonne Dennington.

Thank You All

77477905R00101

Made in the USA
Lexington, KY
29 December 2017